国际和平城市
丛书
International Cities
of Peace

国家出版基金项目
江苏省"十四五"重点图书出版规划项目
侵华日军南京大屠杀遇难同胞纪念馆资助项目

日本
广岛

HIRO-SHIMA

Japan

International Cities of Peace

Series Editor: Liu Cheng
Associate Editors: Ling Xi   Chen Junfeng

Lu Deting

南京师范大学出版社

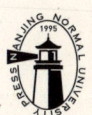

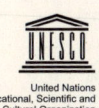

United Nations
Educational, Scientific and
Cultural Organization

UNESCO Chair on Peace Studies
Nanjing University
People's Republic of China

图书在版编目（CIP）数据

日本·广岛 = Hiroshima, Japan：英文 / 陆德婷著
. -- 南京：南京师范大学出版社，2022.10
（国际和平城市丛书 / 刘成主编）
ISBN 978-7-5651-5490-4

Ⅰ.①日… Ⅱ.①陆… Ⅲ.①广岛—概况—英文 Ⅳ.①K931.3

中国版本图书馆 CIP 数据核字（2022）第 198215 号

丛 书 名	国际和平城市丛书
丛书主编	刘 成
丛书副主编	凌 曦　陈俊峰
书　　名	Hiroshima, Japan
著　者	陆德婷
策划编辑	徐 蕾　郑海燕
责任编辑	王雅琼
书籍设计	瀚清堂
出版发行	南京师范大学出版社
地　　址	江苏省南京市玄武区后宰门西村 9 号（邮编：210016）
电　　话	(025)83598712（编辑部）83598919（总编办）83598412（营销部）
网　　址	http://press.njnu.edu.cn
电子信箱	nspzbb@njnu.edu.cn
照　　排	南京私书坊文化传播有限公司
印　　刷	上海雅昌艺术印刷有限公司
开　　本	889 毫米 ×1194 毫米　1/32
印　　张	7.25
版　　次	2022 年 10 月第 1 版　2022 年 10 月第 1 次印刷
书　　号	ISBN 978-7-5651-5490-4
定　　价	50.00 元
出 版 人	张志刚

* 南京师大版图书若有印装问题请与销售商调换
* 版权所有　侵犯必究

Foreword by Series Editor

This book series, International Cities of Peace, Volume I, introduces five cities, which have one thing in common that they have all experienced the trauma of war in their history, and the collective memories have endured from one generation to the next. So, history must be kept in mind. Only by looking back on past sufferings and using history as a mirror can we prevent such historical tragedies from occurring again. It is absolutely vital to recognize and remember the historical trauma, but how we remember it may affect its authenticity and how long we will keep it in mind. According to history, building peace is the best remedy for remembering and recovering from the past suffering. When the traumatic memory of a city is transformed into a common human memory, we can understand the past disasters in a new way beyond stereotyped political memory. Only this can enable the traumatic history to be linked to the future peace, which can promote the reconciliation between the former hostile parties, and boost hope to the establishment of a community with a shared future for mankind. History indicates that reconciliation means not only exchanging our views and experiences of the past, but also a process of mutually creating new ideas for the future and sharing new experiences. In this way, reconciliation is a thought and a power that meets our mutual needs, which can be developed by building cities of peace with the legacy bequeathed by the war. That is why we wrote these books.

All the five cities of the book series are actively engaged in building a culture of peace. Nanjing, the first International City of Peace in China, held an international peace forum on positive peace; Dresden reflects on the war experience of Germany and strengthens domestic and international reconciliation; Hiroshima leads non-governmentally the anti-nuclear peace movement in Japan; Warsaw promotes the reconciliation dialogue that has led to a shared historical memory both inside and outside Poland; Coventry is the benchmark for British reconciliation. At the same time, the study of war memory is undergoing changes in three dimensions: shifts from the hero memory to the traumatic memory, from the memory of a victorious country to the memory of all the wounded countries, and from the domestic historical memory of a country to historical memory shared by many countries. Our belief is that the memory of war will be ultimately eclipsed by the memory of peace, as more and more cities work towards building cities of peace and thus form a global network of peace cities.

The five cities have their own characteristics in building a city of peace. Their practice of building peace has proven the truth that "There is no way to peace; peace is the way". Cities of peace all share a common purpose, promoting the culture of peace advocated by UNESCO, that is, working to build peace through conflict prevention, mediation and transformation; providing peace education on non-violence, tolerance, acceptance, respect and sustainable development; promoting intercultural dialogue and reconciliation. To build a city of peace requires the joint efforts of governments, universities, social groups, non-government organizations and citizens from all countries and regions around the world, for it needs to incorporate elements of peace in historical records, memories and heritage. It can be achieved in many ways, such as conflict prevention, peace-keeping, peace-building, peace research, peace education, and all peace activities that promote urban progress and prosperity as well as world peace and development.

This book series rests on its disciplinary foundation, Peace Studies. With the only UNESCO Chair on Peace Studies in China, Nanjing University is widely recognized as the center of China's Peace Studies. The development of China's Peace Studies has received great help from many institutions and individuals around the world. Without their support, Peace Studies would not have developed in China, and these books would not have been published, either. This book series took ten years to compile, experiencing ups and downs along the way, and finally came out. All the authors, translators and editors have done their best to bring out these books against all the odds, and make them authentic, scholarly, innovative, and readable at the same time.

This book series is an attempt to understand how cultural trauma and historical memory affect us. We sincerely welcome readers to point out and correct the defects and mistakes in these books.

Liu Cheng
Professor, School of History, Nanjing University
Chairholder of UNESCO Chair on Peace Studies
August 2022

Contents

001

Foreword by Series Editor

006

Introduction

008

Chapter 1   **Originating from a City of Water**
- Geographical Features   012
- Historical Development   025
- Sociocultural Environment   028

036

Chapter 2   **Falling into a City of Ashes**
- Transforming into a Military Capital   040
- The Hiroshima Atomic Bombing   062
- The Aftermath of the Hiroshima Atomic Bombing   078

086

Chapter 3   **Striving for Peace from the Grassroots**
- Anti-War Movement   090
- Anti-Nuclear Weapons Movement   095
- Peace Movement   106

Chapter 4   Building up a City of Peace

- Establishment of Legislation for Peace   139
- Construction of Space for Peace   144
- Development of Ritual for Peace   174

Chapter 5   Revisiting Hiroshima through a Peace Studies Lens

- Peace Education and Peace Research   184
- "Pacifism" without Peace   198
- From Negative Peace to Positive Peace   214

Conclusion

Main Bibliography

Afterword

Introduction

Throughout history, Hiroshima has been changing its identities. Before the Meiji Period (1868-1912), it was known as a City of Water, enjoying great geographical advantages that nourished the lives of Hiroshima. However, during the Meiji Period, Hiroshima was transformed into a military capital by Imperial Japan and its military significance was greatly strengthened following the progress of Japan's aggression in Asia. Eventually on 6 August 1945, the city was attacked by the U.S. with an atomic bomb. In a flash, it turned into a city of ashes and was once estimated that no life would grow for 75 years.

War is dreadful but life is wonderful. War brings death but life brings peace. Miraculously, flowers and trees were back to life the following year. They brought the people and the city tremendous hope and courage to get through their long-term recovery from the atomic bombing. Such exuberant vitality from the grassroots was the main driving force during the process of reconstructing Hiroshima into an international city of peace, which has been persistently striving for the elimination of nuclear weapons worldwide.

Overall, the book explores the long journey of what Hiroshima had been like before it was devastated by the atomic bombing, and how it had itself restored from the severely scorched plain and rebuilt into a notable city of peace. Furthermore, a revisit is made through the lens of Peace Studies to encourage Hiroshima to be as proactive as its role played in leading the abolishment of nuclear weapons to restore relationships with its Asian neighbors.

Chapter 1
Originating from a City of Water

Geographical Features

As an island country, Japan consists of thousands of islands, among which Hokkaido, Honshu, Kyushu, Shikoku, and Okinawa are claimed to be its main islands. Situated in the southwest of Japan, Hiroshima prefecture is located in the center of Chugoku Region on Honshu. Bounded to the north by the Chugoku Mountains, the prefecture is generally mountainous with rivers producing rich plains near the coast. Thanks to the Chugoku Mountains that block the cold wind from the Japan Sea, the prefecture is blessed with mild weather throughout the year. To the south, the prefecture borders the Seto Inland Sea, an area dotted with countless islands, large and small, creating a panorama of island beauty [Fig.1-1]. Such geographical advantages make the area ideal for coastal shipping and fishing industries, as well as heavy industries such as shipbuilding.

Many of the islands in the Seto Inland Sea embrace distinct historical, cultural, and industrial backgrounds. Among them, the most well-known island is Itsukushima (or Miyajima) Island, for its Itsukushima Shrine that was originally built in the 6th century, with its floating torii gate on the sea—today a UNESCO World Heritage [Fig.1-2, Fig.1-3].

Fig.1-1 Panoramic view of Hiroshima city and Seto Inland Sea

Fig.1-2 Itsukushima Shrine in Aki province by Utagawa Hiroshige in 1852-1858

Fig.1-3 **Itsukushima Shrine Torii during high tide**

In Japanese, Itsukushima means "island dedicated to kami (god in Japanese)". In fact, the island itself is also considered as a kami, which explains why the shrine was built on the outskirts of the island. To maintain its sanctity, trees may not be cut for lumber. Deer that are considered messengers of kami roam freely on the island. Mount Misen, being the highest mountain on the island, together with its cherry blossom and momiji maple leaves, is renowned throughout Japan. To showcase the tradition and holy spirits of the island, the Shrine and the surrounding temples on the island have been hosting various festivals throughout the history.

Originally, Itsukushima Shrine was a pure Shinto shrine. To ensure its purity, commoners were not allowed to set foot on it for a long period of history. Both the Shrine and the Torii were built over the water, since separating from the land somehow demonstrates the sanctity. The Kanji character "厳"(itsuku), meaning to carry out cleaning practice such as ritual washing and bathing before kami worship, is also considered to ensure purity, which is a major conceptual focus of Shinto or Shintoism. Originated in Japan, Shinto is often seen as a belief in kami, the supernatural entities at the center of the religion. Metaphysically, kami are not deemed different from humanity, so it is possible for humans to become kami. During the Meiji Period, as the government's influence on shrines grew stronger, citizens were encouraged to worship the emperor as a kami. Itsukushima Shrine, one of the most sacred Shinto shrines, also underwent a major renovation to symbolize the absolute loyalty dedicated to the emperor. Borrowing this symbolic meaning, two Imperial Japanese Navy ships that respectively played its key role in the Sino-Japanese War of 1894-1895 (First Sino-Japanese War) and Japanese War of Aggression against China (Second Sino-Japanese War, 1931-1945), were named after the island. They are the cruiser Itsukushima and the minelayer Itsukushima.

Among other islands, Kurahashi Island (used to be called Nagato Island) is famous for its shipbuilding industry. Starting from building wooden ships for missions to the Tang Dynasty, the industry reached its peak in the middle of the Edo Period (1603-1868). Shimokamakari Island, since the Edo Period, has served as a center of marine traffic with ships coming and going, facilitating commerce, and creating prosperity to the area. Osakikami Island is well-known for its cultivation of fruits: blueberries, lemons, mikan oranges, while Hashiri Island and Atata Island enjoy a thriving fishing industry. All together, these ensure the flourishing of the prefecture and the peacefulness of the lives, just as the prefectural emblem tells harmony [Fig.1-4].

Fig.1-4 Emblem of Hiroshima prefecture. Designed from the first character of "Hiroshima" in its Japanese character—"ヒ"(hi), the emblem that has a circular shape represents the harmony and connectedness of the lives in Hiroshima

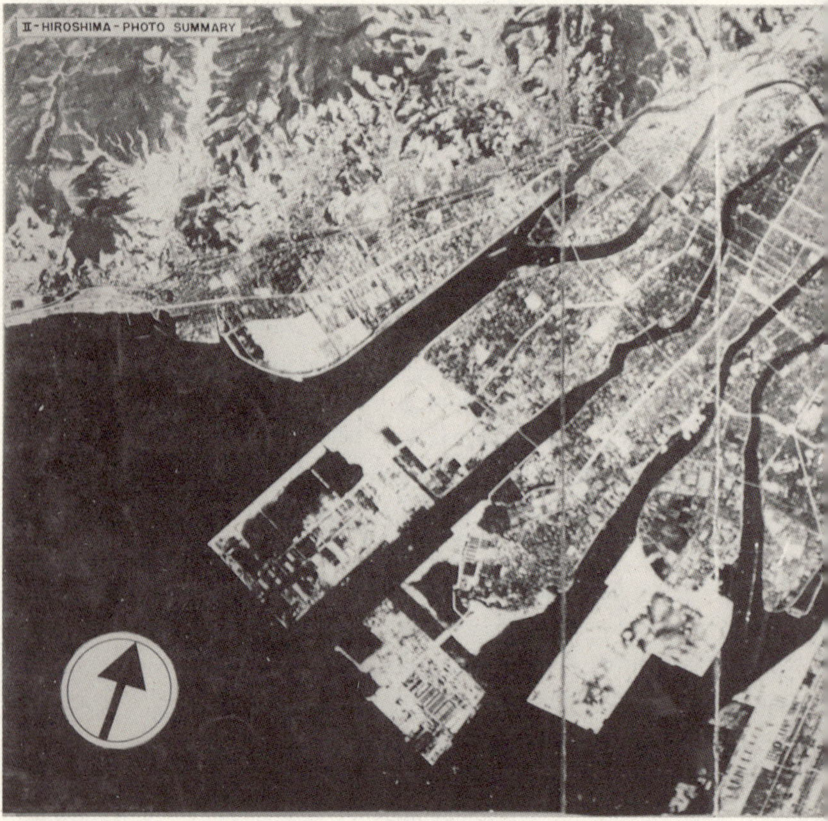

As the capital and largest city of Hiroshima prefecture, Hiroshima city also enjoys a rich natural environment and is blessed by a generally warm climate, being nestled between lush green Chugoku Mountains to the north and tranquil Seto Inland Sea in the south. Sitting on the delta where the Ota River meets the Seto Inland Sea, the city is almost entirely flat and only slightly above sea level. With six rivers (used to be seven) flowing through its center dividing it into six islets that project fingerlike into the Seto Inland Sea [Fig.1-5], Hiroshima is also known as the City of Water.

Fig.1-5 Hiroshima before A-bomb attack, April 1945

Fig.1-6 Momiji around Mitaki-dera (Tahoto)

Passing down from the fertile Chugoku Mountains, the rivers enrich the lives of Hiroshima. During spring, there is a colorful profusion of flowers along the banks of rivers. While in fall, momiji maple leaves spread over a vast area of the city as if they were on fire, bursting with bold autumn gold, yellow and red colors [Fig.1-6]. Having long been a symbol of Hiroshima, momiji maple leaf often appears in traditional paintings and block prints, depicted with the deer of Itsukushima Island. Hiroshima's most famous souvenir, the momiji manju cake [Fig.1-7], also takes the shape of this famous leaf. Embracing both mountain and sea, Hiroshima is also a paradise for various kinds of birds, as well as a breeding base for oysters that have been farmed there for more than four centuries.

Fig.1-7 Momiji manju cake

A pleasing feature of the City of Water is the considerable number of bridges, which strengthens the city's waterway transportation and brings the city prosperity. As early as Mori settled in the castle town, the construction of bridges had already begun. Well-known bridges, such as the Enkou Bridge [Fig.1-8], Motoyasu Bridge [Fig.1-9] and Hongawa Bridge [Fig.1-10] were all built during that period though in wood structures. Another significant bridge was the Aioi Bridge [Fig.1-11]. Originally built in the Meiji Period, it was the junction of the Motoyasu Bridge and Hongawa Bridge, as well as the key bridge providing transportation connectivity to the most flourishing Nakajima area. But as wood structures could not endure severe disasters, after entering the Taisho Period (1912-1926), most of the bridges were reconstructed into reinforced concrete ones and some were able to maintain their structures till today.

Fig.1-8 Enkou Bridge during the Taisho Period

Fig.1-9 Motoyasu Bridge during the Taisho Period

Fig.1-10 Hongawa Bridge during the Taisho Period

Fig.1-11 Aioi Bridge during the Taisho Period

Fig.1-12 City view of Hiroshima from Futabayama during the Taisho Period

Being surrounded by the Chugoku Mountains, the city also enjoys a greenery environment where there are many parks, gardens, temples, and shrines settling in, promoting the well-being of the local lives [Fig.1-12, Fig.1-13]. The most renowned and gorgeous garden is Shukkeien [Fig.1-14], which is said to be the garden that captures the beauty of West Lake in Hangzhou, China. Located in the center of Hiroshima near Hiroshima Castle, it was built by Asano during the Edo Period as a villa garden. The lake in Shukkeien is always filled with carp, therefore, Hiroshima Castle is also affectionately called Carp Castle. Since 1913, the gardens have been opened to the public. What's more, those that were close to the sea, such as Nakashima Park [closed during the Showa Period (1926-1989)] [Fig.1-15], also served as beach parks where people could enjoy relaxing on the beach.

Fig.1-13 Cherry blossoms in Choujuen, Nishihaku, Hiroshima, during the Taisho Period

Fig.1-14 Asano's Garden (today's Shukkeien) during the Taisho Period

Fig.1-15 Nakashima Park during the Taisho Period

Historical Development

In prehistoric times, most of today's Hiroshima city was submerged in the Seto Inland Sea, although earthenware relics from the Jomon Period indicate human activity in certain areas. Around the late 6th to early 7th century, the area became a cultural bridge between Kyushu, further to the west, and Kinki, the modern-day Kansai region, with trade routes through the mountains and along the coast. At that time, eastern Hiroshima was known as Bingo province while western Hiroshima was known as Aki province.

During the Sengoku Period (Warring States Period, 1467-1573) of Japan's feudal era, the Mori clan ruled over Aki province, Bingo province, and the rest of the modern-day Chugoku region. In the late 16th century, Terumoto Mori, the regional warlord, decided to build a castle from which to rule over his extensive domain. Taking advantage of its pivotal geographical location, Mori settled on the delta of Ota River that flows through the area into the Seto Inland Sea. At the time, the area was referred to as Gokamura (Five villages), due to the five lobes of the delta. When the castle was tentatively completed in 1591, Mori renamed the area Hiroshima: Hiro for his ancestor Oeno Hiromoto, and Shima after Motonaga Fukushima, who helped Mori select the site for the castle. Hiroshima in Japanese means "wide island", which aptly describes the island in the center of the delta on which Hiroshima Castle was built.

Fig.1-16 Hiroshima Castle during the Taisho Period

After being lord of Hiroshima Castle for 10 years, Terumoto Mori was defeated at the battle of Sekigahara in 1600 and was forced to abandon Hiroshima. The Tokugawa shogunate, who gained control after the battle, awarded Hiroshima Castle to his ally Masanori Fukushima. Fukushima ruled Hiroshima for about 20 years and was reassigned to the backwoods of Nagano since he displeased Tokugawa. As a result, the Hiroshima domain once again welcomed its new governor Nagaakira Asano, who ruled for more than 10 generations. Over the next few centuries, under Asano rule, Hiroshima expanded to become a bustling Edo castle town and was a center for fishing, commerce, and arts in the Chugoku region [Fig.1-16].

During the Meiji Restoration, the administration system of local municipalities was changed, where the feudal domains were replaced with modern prefectures. The old towns and villages were abolished, and the entire country was divided into large districts and subdivided into smaller ones. Accordingly, Aki province was abolished, and the Hiroshima domain was soon reformed into Hiroshima prefecture. The castle town was subdivided into four small districts. Following the establishment of the new system of municipality in 1888, Hiroshima officially gained its city status in 1889. Subsequently, following the Taisho Period, the local economy greatly shifted from rural to urban industries, which led to the city's continuous growth. Eventually, it transformed into an economically and culturally important city of Japan.

Sociocultural Environment

Taking advantage of its geographical location, Hiroshima, since its founding as a castle town, has been enjoying a flourishing local life. When the area was called Gokamura, there had been nothing more than a group of tiny fishing villages. After the settlement of the Mori clan, Hiroshima was instantly transformed into a bustling town. Retainers, merchants, and artisans moved in. Bridges and roads were constructed. Rivers running through the town were utilized for water transport, connecting the town with the Seto Inland Sea. Two canals were built, the Hirataya in the east, and the Seito in the west, to serve as harbors. Regular markets were run by traders, selling vegetables, fruits, and processed farm products, such as straw mats, tatami mats, and baskets made of bamboo brought in from places on the upper course of the Ota River.

When Fukushima's rule began, Hiroshima continued to develop. Communities were organized under magistrates, neighborhood groups were set up to control the populace, and each group had an appointed senior leader. Later under the rule of Asano, new land was added to create new housing areas by filling in shallow areas of the bay and leveling the mountains.

Thereafter, the castle town expanded to have more than 35 new towns and villages. The population of the newly established settlements exceeded 48,000. Together with the original city dwellers of an estimated 20,000 samurai and civilians residing in temples and shrines, the total population of the new town was nearly 70,000.

With Hiroshima being the largest castle town on the coast of the Seto Inland Sea, Hongawa and Motoyasu rivers of Hiroshima were always bustling with ships from other parts of Japan. The castle town, at that period, enjoyed lively commerce. Numerous local products from neighboring areas, such as cotton grown in the coastal regions; jute, paper, bamboo wares and vegetables from the Ota River basin; and seaweed, oysters, and other marine products from Hiroshima Bay, were all transported to the area near Hiroshima Castle where they were consolidated and shipped off to Kyoto and Osaka.

Following the Meiji Restoration, rule by the shogunate was ended, and all power returned to the emperor, with the goal of reforming and modernizing Japan by combining Western technology with traditional Japanese values. In order to take steps forward to a modernized city,

Fig.1-17 Hondori Street, during the pre-war Showa Period

Fig.1-18 Shinten Chi, during the pre-war Showa Period

Fig.1-19 The crossroad of "Kamiyacho" in 1938

further urbanization in Hiroshima was stimulated. The sewage system was greatly developed, and gas and electricity were widely popularized. The Kabe Line and the Geibi Line were successively built, which resulted in train transportation superseding shipping on the Ota River. Streetcars were introduced and became the main form of transportation within the city. Brick and reinforced concrete buildings appeared one after another, largely changing the cityscape [Fig.1-17 to Fig.1-19].

Fig.1-20 Hiroshima Prefectural Industrial Promotion Hall during the pre-war Showa Period

Take Nakajima District, once the city's busiest downtown commercial and residential district for example. During the Edo Period, Nakajima was a thriving commercial center where products came by sea and were sold elsewhere by land. After entering the Meiji Period, it developed into the political, administrative, and commercial heart of Hiroshima. During the early years of the Showa Period, there were movie theaters, restaurants, kimono shops, general stores and various businesses lining the streets of the district. The Hiroshima Prefectural Industrial Promotion Hall [Fig.1-20] was also located in the district, introducing products from different areas to promote local commerce as well as serving as a facility for art and education exhibitions. Unfortunately, due to the atomic bombing, both Nakajima District and the Promotion Hall were seriously destroyed. Today, Nakajima District is home to the Hiroshima Peace Memorial Park, and the Promotion Hall is recognized as the Atomic Bomb Dome or Genbaku Dome (hereinafter referred to as "A-bomb Dome").

Simultaneously, Western culture and lifestyle were also introduced and popularized in Hiroshima. Everything from men's haircuts to drinking milk, from the solar calendar to ballroom dancing, made the city life lively. Additionally, following the order of the Meiji Government to seek knowledge from all over the world to strengthen the emperor's rule, the educational system was improved nationwide. Learning from the West, compulsory education towards the public, both boys and girls, as well as higher education for industrial development was encouraged. Along with the construction of banks and hospitals, public schools and language institutes were also established in Hiroshima. Back then, the state-run Hiroshima Higher School and the Hiroshima Higher Normal School [Fig.1-21] were both ranked as top schools in Japan, which granted Hiroshima the center of education [Fig.1-22].

Fig.1-21 Hiroshima Higher Normal School during the Meiji Period

Fig.1-22 Hiroshima Prefectural Education Center during the pre-war Showa Period

In short, as one of the first cities having gained its city status, Hiroshima experienced its dramatic transformation from a fishing village into an economically, politically, culturally, and educationally significant center of Japan. The local citizens had been enjoying a peaceful life where both Japanese and Western cultures and values could be appreciated. But this did not last long. As the heavy industrialization was further stimulated during the war, the city was turned into a military capital that contributed to Imperial Japan's invasion in Asia. Military supplies became its initial priority.

2

Chapter 2

Falling into a City of Ashes

Transforming into a Military Capital

Since the early Meiji Period when "Datsua Nyuo" (Leave Asia, Enter Europe) was put forward by Yukichi Fukuzawa [Fig.2-1], one of modern Japan's leading thinkers, Japan had embarked on the road of capitalism and gradually developed into a militaristic empire. Together with the slogan "Fukoku Kyohei" (a phrase from the ancient Chinese historical work *Zhan Guo Ce*, meaning enriching nation and strengthening army), the modernization of the Japanese

Fig.2-1 Yukichi Fukuzawa, around 1891

Army and Navy was carried out by the military-led national government modeled after those of France and Germany. In the late Meiji Period, as militarism further dominated the political and social life of the entire Japanese nation, there came domestic conflicts. As a solution to ease the situation, expansionism overseas was proposed, which eventually caused tens of millions of Asians that were estimated to have been killed by Japanese invaders.

In the second half of the 19th century, Japan launched and participated in multiple wars of aggression against the Korean Peninsula, China, and other East Asian neighbors. Following the end of World War I (1914-1918), the balance of power among the imperialist nations was significantly altered. It also worsened the crisis on the development of Japanese imperialism. The Japanese military began to realize that future wars must be backed up by strong productivity, which demanded an abundance of supplies and advanced technologies. As a result, resource-poor Japan made its decision to invade China to seize new territory for resource extraction and settlement of surplus population. Aspiring to this bold expansionist vision, the military indoctrinated the populace with ultra-nationalist ideals and affirmed their loyalty to the emperor and the military, attempting to establish a fascist regime dictated by the military.

In February 1936, with the establishment of fascist military led by the Hirota Cabinet, the emperor-system fascism (or Japanese fascism) was further confirmed, accelerating the pace of waging war against China. On 7 July 1937, Japan provoked the Lugouqiao Incident (also the Marco Polo Bridge Incident), which eventually led to the Japanese War of Aggression against China on a full scale. In November 1938, Imperial Japan made an official announcement of a New Order in East Asia in order to build a so-called "Greater East Asia Co-Prosperity Sphere". In December 1941, the Japanese Imperial Army attacked Pearl Harbor attempting to prevent the U.S. Pacific fleet from interfering with its planned military operation in resource-rich Southeast Asia. In response, the U.S. declared war on Japan, and the Pacific War (1941-1945) broke out.

Till then, Japan had waged the largest-scale war of aggression in the modern history of East Asia, mobilized all resources of its military, capital, and labor to fight what was called a "total war". Other resources, energy, labor, and military forces Japan seized from the Korean Peninsula, China, and Southeast Asia were used as its foundation for further expansion. Consequently, Imperial Japan turned out to be one of the major enemies of the World Anti-Fascism War. Throughout its aggression, Japan blatantly violated international laws, carrying out organized biological and chemical warfare; murdering, maiming and ill-treating prisoners of war and civilian internees; forcing labor under inhumane conditions; indiscriminately bombing against civilians; and committing crimes of sexual violence against women including its establishment of "Comfort Women" System, etc. Hiroshima city, serving as the military capital during the wartime, surely contributed a lot to Japan's aggressive wars overseas.

Fully Equipped Military City

At the dawn of the Meiji Period, Hiroshima city took on national importance, and it grew into an economic, industrial, and military center of Japan. Enjoying an advantageous geographical location, Hiroshima was chosen by the Meiji Government to strengthen its military power. Around 1871, the First Detached Garrison of Western Japan was set up in Hiroshima Castle. Two years later, the Hiroshima Garrison of the Fifth Military District was established with Hiroshima and other nine prefectures under its administration. Renamed the Fifth Division in 1886, they were the first to be sent to the front when the Sino-Japanese War of 1894-1895 broke out. At the time of the Russo-Japanese War (1904-1905), new military installations were built one after another inside and outside Hiroshima Castle, steadily reinforcing Hiroshima as a military capital.

Apart from the strengthened armed forces, the construction of Ujina Port (now Hiroshima Port) and railways also contributed to Hiroshima's functioning as a key military city of Japan [Fig.2-2]. On 25 July 1894, as the Sino-Japanese War of 1894-1895 broke out, a railway line from the Hiroshima station to Ujina Port was constructed right away to enhance the efficiency of military transportation. Surprisingly completed within 16 days, the railway helped Hiroshima become the primary military transportation hub for dispatching troops and supplies to the front line in China. In 1903, the Kure Line was also opened for military use, providing direct rail access from the Kure naval port to Hiroshima, which solidified Hiroshima's role as a principal military base during the Russo-Japanese War.

Fig.2-2 Ujina Port during the Meiji Period

The outbreak of the Sino-Japanese War of 1894-1895 not only brought improvement to land-sea transportation facilities, but also strengthened the political significance of Hiroshima. At the time, thousands of Japanese castles either were dismantled or fell into disrepair under the 1873 Ordinance for Keeping and Disposal of Castles and Selection of Military Posts, but Hiroshima Castle was allowed to remain standing and eventually converted into a military facility.

On 15 September 1894, the Japanese Government moved temporarily to Hiroshima [Fig.2-3], and Emperor Meiji maintained Military Headquarters at Hiroshima Castle from then to 27 April 1895 [Fig.2-4]. Later the first round of talks between Chinese and Japanese representatives to end the war was also held in Hiroshima, from 1 February to 4 February 1895.

Fig.2-3 *Emperor Meiji arrives in Hiroshima*

Fig.2-4 Military Headquarters at Hiroshima Castle during the pre-war Showa Period

During the period when Hiroshima served as the temporary capital, the city was prosperous and busy with distinguished government officials coming and going, new soldiers leaving for the front and wounded ones returning, and traders gathering from all around Japan. After entering the Showa Period, as the post-WWI recession continued, the Imperial Japanese Army turned their attention to the expansion in the Asian mainland regardless of civilians' groaning under oppression. Triggered by the September 18 Incident in 1931, the Japanese War of Aggression against China started and eventually escalated into a full-scale invasion of China. The Fifth Division based in Hiroshima was sent from Ujina Port, as the advance party joining the battlefield on the Chinese continent.

With the progress of the war the requirement for military supplies increased, which further developed the heavy industries in Hiroshima. In 1938, the enactment of the National Mobilization Act granted the military supplies the highest priority. Consequently, military facilities were newly established and largely expanded, and military industries such as shipbuilding (including the Mitsubishi Shipbuilding) and metal industries were greatly promoted.

Closely Surrounded Naval Bases

About 20 kilometers from Hiroshima, there lies a port and major shipbuilding city named Kure. With a strong industrial heritage, Kure hosts the second-oldest naval dockyard in Japan and remains an important base for the Japan Maritime Self-Defense Force (JMSDF). Within the sheltered Inland Sea, Kure was recognized to be of strategic importance in controlling the sea lanes around western Japan. Thus, in 1889, Kure Naval District was established for the defense of western Japan. Until the end of World War II (1931-1945), Kure city served as the headquarters of the Kure Naval District. Acting as Japan's single-largest naval base and arsenal, most of the city's industry and workforce were employed in the service of the naval installations, munitions factories and associated support functions.

In 1920, the Japanese Navy established its main submarine base, together with a submarine warfare training school in Kure. An air wing was established in 1932, and a telecommunications center in 1937. At the time of the attack on Pearl Harbor in 1941, Kure Naval District played a key role. Accordingly, in the final stage of the war, it came under sustained aerial bombardment by the United States Navy and United States Army Air Forces. It ultimately culminated in the Bombing of Kure in June and July 1945, with many of the facilities being heavily destroyed.

After the war, the Kure area came under occupation by Australian and British forces during the occupation of Japan and was largely demilitarized. But a small portion of military facilities continued to be occupied by the JMSDF and today those preserved have been part of the JMSDF Kure Museum, which is located next to the Yamato Museum. The Yamato Museum, also known as the Kure Maritime Museum, opened on 23 April 2005. It displays the large model ship—Yamato [Fig.2-5], the flagship of the Japanese Combined Fleet in World War II that was sunk south of the Japanese island of Kyushu in 1945. The museum is located where the battleship was completed.

Fig.2-5 Imperial Japanese Navy's Battleship Yamato running full-power trials in Sukumo Bay, 30 October 1941

Close to Kure, there is a roughly Y-shaped island named Etajima, which now serves as the base of the JMSDF and houses the First Technical School and the Officer Candidates School. Relocated to Etajima in 1888, the Imperial Japanese Naval Academy (now the JMSDF Officer Candidates School) [Fig.2-6] had its candidates go through intense physical, mental, and technical military training to withstand the demanding conditions of battles. For example, part of the physical training was practicing long-distance swimming from Etajima to Itsukushima and climbing Mount Misen on Itsukushima. Since the Meiji Period when the emperor was made a kami, training on Itsukushima, the sacred island dedicated to kami, also helped cultivate a sense of absolute loyalty to the emperor among the candidates. Until it was closed by the

Fig.2-6 JMSDF Officer Candidate School, which was formerly the Imperial Japanese Naval Academy, built in 1893

Allied Forces in 1945, the school had trained many prominent officers who were later famous in Japan's naval history. Notorious ones who actively participated in World War II, such as Isoroku Yamamoto, Kiyoshi Hasegawa, and Shigeyoshi Inoue, were all graduates of the school.

Located inside the JMSDF Etajima Base, there is the Museum of Naval History, covering Japan's naval history chronologically from the late 19th century to the end of the Imperial Japanese Navy in 1945, with a focus on its accomplishments and victories. Whereas the Navy's disastrous defeat at Midway in 1942, the series of the naval losses up to the sinking of the Battleship Yamato in April 1945 and the loss of Okinawa in June 1945 were barely depicted.

The museum has two large rooms, displaying exhibits related to the Navy's special attack forces of planes, midget submarines, and manned torpedoes. The first room is dedicated to the Japanese Navy's Special Attack Units. On the wall, there is a long bronze tablet inscribed with 2,633 names of members of the Kamikaze special attack corps and the Kaiten human torpedo force who died. Following the unfavorable progress of the war, suicide mission vehicles were developed in the Japanese Special Attack Units. For the Navy, this meant Kamikaze planes, Shinyo speedboats, Kaiten human torpedoes, and Fukuryu suicide divers [Fig.2-7].

The second room on the Navy's Special Attack Units presents the leaders of the Kamikaze operations and about 150 last letters and wills by Kamikaze pilots. All the descriptions of the Kamikaze seem to honor them rather than to critically evaluate their actions. However, in the eyes of those whose motherland had been invaded by Japan, the Kamikaze attack was a desperate act of Imperial Japan before it was defeated. The young and fanatical pilots were prisoners of both militarism and imperialism, who served as war machines during Japan's aggression.

Fig.2-7 Corporal Yukio Araki, holding a puppy, with four other Kamikaze pilots of the 72nd Shinbu Squadron at Bansei, Kagoshima, 26 May 1945. Araki died the following day, at the age of 17, in a suicide attack near Okinawa

Barely Known Poison Gas Island

Okunoshima is a small island located three kilometers off the southern coast of Tadanoumi Port in Takehara city, Hiroshima prefecture [Fig.2-8]. Surrounded by the quiet Seto Inland Sea, the island offers enjoyment of watching various flowers blooming from season to season. Today, it is recognized as a popular vacation resort dotted with tennis courts, bicycle paths, palm trees and a modest four-story hotel. Since there are numerous feral rabbits roaming the island, Okunoshima is also affectionately called Usagi Shima (Rabbit Island).

However, today's resort island was deemed as a secret poison gas factory during the war and had once been removed from maps. Since the 1890s, military facilities, such as forts and cannons had been installed on the island to defend against foreign invasions. As the power of chemical weapons was widely acknowledged during World War I, in 1918, the Imperial Japanese Army initiated a secret program to develop chemical weapons in a temporary committee of poison gas. Eventually in 1927, the plan was made to house a plant to manufacture poison gas on Okunoshima, considering it was easy to maintain security on the island and its isolation from the capital and other areas was important in case of accidents.

Directly undertaken by the Army, the plant was fully completed as the Tokyo Second Military Arsenal Tadanoumi Munitions Plant on 19 May 1929 [Fig.2-9]. The facilities expanded rapidly between 1938 and 1940, employing up to 6,000 workers [Fig.2-10]. Back then rabbits were also used in the chemical munitions plant to test the effectiveness of the poison gas. Nevertheless, it was said those rabbits were killed when the plant was demolished and were not related to the rabbits currently on the island. Until the end of World War II, the island served as Japan's only plant for large-scale poison gas production. It produced approximately 6,600 tons of various types of poison gas, such as choking gas, sneezing gas, tear gas and mustard gas [Fig.2-11], of which were largely used in China from the very beginning of the war.

Fig.2-8 Okunoshima from Kurotakiyama, October 2010

Fig.2-9 Boiler plant on Okunoshima, 3 October 1946

Fig.2-10 Japanese arsenal worker in the poison gas factory on Okunoshima, 30 August 1946

Fig.2-11 Containers filled with mustard gas on Okunoshima, 3 August 1946

With Japan's invasion of China in 1937, came the use of chemical and biological weapons against the Chinese. According to a gas soldier's military handbook, poison gas was used 9 times in 1937 and 185 in 1938. There were 465 times in 1939, 259 in 1940, and 48 in 1941. It was employed in China all the way through 1945. The use of poison gas was brought before the League of Nations and evidence was collected, but Japan denied it had used gas until 1984. In 1990, China officially raised its concerns regarding chemical weapons left behind by Japan. In 1997, the Chemical Weapons Convention (CWC) became effective, urging Japan to take full responsibility for destroying all the Abandoned Chemical Weapons (ACW) on Chinese territory. On 30 July 1999, Japan signed a memorandum concerning ACW in China with the Chinese Government. Eventually, activities related to excavation and collection of ACW in China started in 2000.

In accordance with CWC, Japan has an obligation as an Abandoning State to complete the destruction of all ACW left on Chinese territory no later than 15 years after the date of entry into force of the Convention, namely by 2012. However, due to various uncertainties and difficulties to carry out the excavation and collection procedure, the plan for ACW destruction has long been delayed. In February 2012, a consensus was reached between the two governments, where Japan is set to complete destruction activities by the end of 2027. Today, the ACW destruction project in China is still in process.

Japan was one signatory on the 1925 Geneva Protocol which prohibited the use of chemical and biological weapons in the war, but the development and storage of chemical weapons were not banned. Japan went to all lengths to ensure the secrecy of constructing chemical munitions plants on the island. Local people and potential employees were not told what the plant was manufacturing, and everything was kept strictly secret. The island itself was even removed from Japanese maps in 1938, leaving only a blank sea, and it did not reappear officially until 1947. Immediately after World War II, the island was taken over by the U.S. Army who oversaw the destruction of the gas factory. Secretly, the plant was burnt, and the disposal of the remaining poison gas took place on the island and in the surrounding waters. Most were disposed of by ocean dumping off the coast near the island. Some were also buried under the former bomb proof shelters left on the island and the rest were incinerated at sea.

The number of people who engaged in this secret project was recorded to be over 6,500, including factory workers, office staff, Joshi Teishintai (Women's Volunteer Corps), mobilized students and Fujin Kai (Women's Association), etc. All were told to be silent about the project. However, since the working conditions were extremely harsh, many workers suffered from toxic-exposure related illnesses. Several decades later, victims who used to work in the plant established the Poison Gas Workers' Association, seeking compensation from the Japanese Government for the injuries they suffered while making all kinds of poison gas during the war. Every autumn, family members of poison gas victims gather on the island and hold a memorial ceremony.

Fig.2-12 Poison Gas Museum on the island

In 1988, a Poison Gas Museum opened on the island, displaying work clothes and datebooks from the former factory workers and equipment used to manufacture poison gas at that time [Fig.2-12]. While presenting the dreadful history of the island, the museum is also regarded as an educational base helping to think about peace, which is based on the realization of both facets of victimization and perpetration in the war [Fig.2-13]. Regarding the exhibits of the museum, it lays its focus on the victimization of the workers who used to work in the factory. Unfortunately, there is not much depicting the sufferings of Chinese victims of chemical weapons.

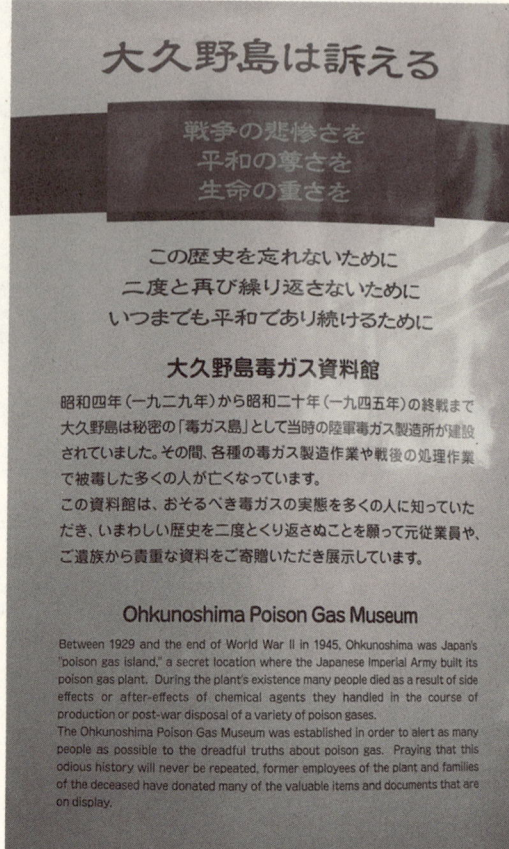

Fig.2-13 General introduction of the Poison Gas Museum

In addition to the Poison Gas Museum, there are other Japanese military ruins preserved on the island. For example, three complete sets of Meiji-Period gun batteries, a gutted power plant shell, disappearing searchlight positions, and poison gas storehouses everywhere from one end of Okunoshima to the other. All these ruins offer a clear picture of the island being supportive for Hiroshima's role as a military capital during the war.

Mobilized Civilians for War Effort

After the outbreak of Japan's full-scale invasion of China, National Mobilization Law (Kokka Sodoin Ho) was enacted on 1 April 1938 to put the national economy of Imperial Japan on a war footing. It provided for government controls over civilian organizations, nationalization of strategic industries, pricing and rationing, and the news media. As a supplement, National Service Draft Ordinance (Kokumin Choyo Rei) was promulgated, which empowered the government to draft civilian workers to ensure an adequate supply of labor in strategic war industries. Under the Law, the National Spiritual Mobilization Movement (Kokumin Seishin Sodoin Undo) was also initiated with its aim to rally the entire nation for a total war effort against China. As a result, the previously existing nationalist organizations became part of the central league of the Movement, playing their leading roles to strengthen patriotism nationwide [Fig.2-14].

As a matter of course, citizens in Hiroshima were no exception. On the day Hiroshima was bombed, it was estimated about 43,000 soldiers were in the city, among whom there were local citizen soldiers. The notorious Fifth Division, which was briefly mentioned in the previous session, was formed in Hiroshima as the Hiroshima Garrison (Hiroshima Chindai). Named after the Hiroshima Castle (also known as Carp Castle/Rijo), its call sign was the Koi (Carp) Division (Koi Heidan). Under the Fifth Division, personnel drafted from Hiroshima formed the Eleventh Infantry Regiment. Throughout its operational history, it participated in the Sino-Japanese War of 1894-1895, the Eight-Nation Alliance's Invasion of China (1900-1901), and the Russo-Japanese War. During the Japanese war of Aggression against China, the Division played a key role in carrying out brutal war crimes on the land of China, such as Beijing, Shanxi, Shandong, and Jiangsu, etc.

Fig.2-14 A poster calling for civilian war efforts, displayed in the Hiroshima Peace Memorial Museum

While men were mobilized for military service, women at home were organized by some women groups, such as Patriotic Women's Association (Aikoku Fujikai), to provide welfare for the bereaved families of the war dead, send off and welcome back soldiers with grand ceremonies as well as prepare relief packages for the soldiers to be sent to the front line. Additionally, many of the local women were drafted to work in the military industries, such as the Army Clothing Depot for military uniform supply, the poison gas plant for chemical weapon production, etc. As Japan's war situation worsened, numerous students from middle schools and girls' high schools were also mobilized to help demolition work in the city to protect military facilities from air raids.

All together with the enormous numbers of military facilities, surrounded naval bases and poison gas island, and mobilized civilians serving the war, ensured Hiroshima's role as a military capital of the nation. Following the attack on Pearl Harbor, a Marine headquarters was set up in Ujina Port, and relevant units were placed on the coast to protect the city. Air defense setup in the city was rapidly strengthened and became obviously stronger than that in other cities. When the military situation turned out to be increasingly worse, the Second General Headquarters was stationed in Hiroshima for commanding the defense of the whole southern Japan, and the highest administrative body commissioned by the central government also moved to Hiroshima. Eventually, Hiroshima became the assembly area for troops.

The Hiroshima Atomic Bombing

No Sign of Surrender

On 7 December 1941, the Empire of Japan launched its attack on Pearl Harbor in Hawaii and plunged into the Pacific War. In the early stages, the Japanese Empire reached its first goal quickly, taking the Philippines, Malaya, Singapore, and the Dutch East Indies (now Indonesia). Civilians were excited about the news of its nation's successive victories but continued to suffer from severe conditions as the war prolonged. In 1942, Japan lost the Battle of Midway and was inflicted devastating damage on its fleet by the U.S. Navy. The following year, it was defeated in the Battle of Guadalcanal, which marked the Allies' transition from defensive operations to offensive ones. Gradually, the U.S. Army seized the strategic initiative in the Pacific Theater from the Imperial Japanese Army.

On 1 December 1943, the Cairo Declaration was jointly released by China, the United States, and the United Kingdom. The three Allies agreed upon future military cooperation against Japan till its unconditional surrender. Following the war, all territories Japan had seized from China since 1914 would be returned and Korea would gain independence. Consequently, the Allied strategic fighting against Japan by sea, land and air began and continued to intensify. In recognition of the unfavorable progress of the war, suicide mission vehicles were developed in the Japanese Special Attack Units, including Kamikaze planes, Shinyo speedboats, Kaiten human torpedoes and Fukuryu suicide divers. Meanwhile the Imperial Japanese Army made quick preparations for the coming decisive battle in the mainland, intending to fight to the bitter end.

Thus, how to force the surrender of Japan and end the war in Asia Pacific became the most serious challenge to the Allied Forces. On 8 May 1945, Germany's unconditional surrender ended the war in Europe, and the Allies turned their full attention to the Asia Pacific. To carry out the planned ground attack of the Japanese homeland, the U.S. forces landed on the island of Okinawa and won the battle in June 1945. However, considering the Japanese troops on Okinawa were so fierce in their defense and the casualties were so appalling, many American strategists suggested an alternative means to conquer mainland Japan, other than a direct costly landing. And the means was the use of atomic bombs.

On 26 July 1945, China, the United States, and the United Kingdom released the Potsdam Declaration, calling for the unconditional surrender of Imperial Japan. As an ultimatum, it stated if Japan did not surrender, it would face "prompt and utter destruction". The declaration offered terms about the eventual form of government for Japan, which are the deprivation of all territories it had seized or occupied, withdrawal of its military force, and accusation of committing war crimes. Upon receiving the declaration, Emperor Hirohito stated it was "acceptable in principle". However, since the declaration left the emperor's status unclear, military leaders opposed to accept arguing that the terms were "too dishonorable", while others preferred to postpone the reply since they still had hope that the Soviet Union would agree to mediate peace. Eventually, on 30 July 1945, Prime Minister Kantaro Suzuki stated that the Japanese policy toward the declaration was "mokusatsu", which was interpreted by the U.S. as "rejection by ignoring". As a result, the decision to drop an atomic bomb on Hiroshima was made.

Hiroshima on 6 August 1945

Around the period when U.S.'s full-scale aerial bomb attacks on mainland Japan was ongoing, people in other cities were suffering both poverty and large air raids, while Hiroshima remained without suffering major damage from air strikes up to 6 August. There were rumors running wild that the enemy had something special for Hiroshima, but no one ever dreamed that the end would come with a single bomb on the morning of 6 August. By 31 July, Little Boy was ready for delivery. On 2 August the order of Hiroshima to be specified as the primary target was given. The raid was set for 6 August.

At approximately 2:00 a.m., on 6 August 1945, a modified American B-29 Superfortress bomber named the Enola Gay left the Pacific Island of Tinian for Hiroshima. The four-engine plane was followed by two observation planes carrying cameras and scientific instruments, which oversaw observing and photographing the explosion. Only the Enola Gay was carrying a bomb named Little Boy [Fig.2-15] that was over 3 meters in length, almost 0.75 meters in diameter. Weighing close to 4.5 tons, the bomb was estimated to have the explosive force of 20,000 tons of TNT. Around 6:00 a.m., Little Boy was fully armed on board the Enola Gay.

In Hiroshima, 6 August began with a bright, cloudless, summer morning. About 7:00 a.m., the Japanese radar detected aircraft heading toward Japan, and the alert was broadcast throughout the Hiroshima area. Soon afterward, a weather plane circled over the city, but there was no sign of bombers. Not much attention was paid and the all-clear was sounded in half an hour. People began their daily work and thought the danger had passed. Many national volunteer corps and

Fig.2-15 A-bomb Little Boy, August 1945

mobilized students were helping the demolition work in the city, to create firebreaks as air-raid protection. At 7:25 a.m., the Enola Gay was cruising over Hiroshima at some 8,000 meters. At 8:09 a.m., the crew of the Enola Gay could see the city appear below and received a message indicating that the weather was good over Hiroshima.

By 8:00 a.m., Japanese radar again detected B-29s heading toward the city. It was said there was no warning at all, while some documents showed that NHK Hiroshima was about to broadcast another air-raid warning right at 8:15 a.m. At precisely 8:15, Enola Gay dropped the Little Boy by parachute from an altitude of 8,500 meters. The T-shaped Aioi Bridge at the junction of the Honkawa and Motoyasu rivers near downtown Hiroshima was the target. But after falling for about 43 seconds, it exploded mid-air in a nuclear eruption about 590 meters above the Shima Surgical Hospital, slightly southeast of the original target and of the Hiroshima Prefectural Industrial Promotion Hall (now known as the A-bomb Dome) [Fig.2-16].

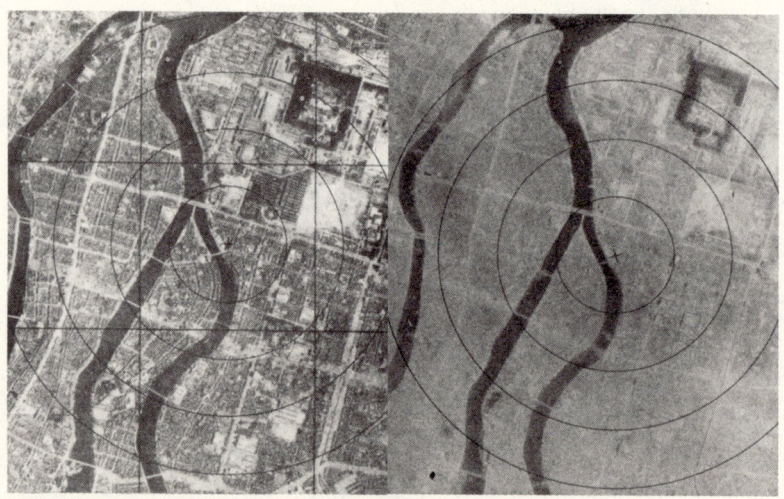

Fig.2-16 Hiroshima before bombing (left) and Hiroshima after bombing and firestorm (right)

At the instant of the explosion, a gigantic fireball of several hundred thousand degrees centigrade formed. And 0.3 seconds later, the fireball attained a temperature on the surface of 7,000 degrees centigrade. Intense thermal radiation was emitted by the fireball for 3 seconds after the explosion, and some continued to be emitted for about 10 seconds. The temperature at the hypocenter, the hypothetical point where the bomb would have hit the ground, reached around 3,000 to 4,000 degrees centigrade (iron melts at 1,536 degrees centigrade). Those exposed to the heat rays within 1 kilometer were killed by intense burn and the rupture of internal organs. Burns were caused to the bodies of those within 3.5 kilometers of the hypocenter, and clothes and wooden houses were ignited. A huge pillar of smoke and debris rose to a height of 9 kilometers within 8 minutes and formed a mushroom-shaped cloud that was visible many miles from the city.

A few seconds after the explosion, the surrounding air expanded enormously, generating a shock wave followed by a powerful blast. At the hypocenter, the blast had a maximum blast pressure of 35 tons per square meter and a maximum wind velocity of 440 meters per second. At 1.3 kilometers from the hypocenter, the blast attained a force of 7 tons per square meter and a wind velocity of 120 meters per second. The explosive wind reached 11 kilometers about 30 seconds after the explosion. The blast stripped people of clothing, tore off burned skin, and ruptured the internal organs of some victims, and it drove glass and other debris into their bodies [Fig.2-17]. Wooden buildings within a radius of 2.3 kilometers were leveled and over half of all such buildings within 3.2 kilometers were destroyed. Even concrete buildings near the hypocenter were smashed by the blast [Fig.2-18].

Fig.2-17 The first two photographs by Yoshihito Matsushige at the west end of Miyuki Bridge just after 11:00 a.m

Fig.2-18 Standing at the hypocenter in October 1945—East: from the left to the right, there stands Chiyoda Insurance Chugoku Branch, Geibi Bank Central Branch, and Sumitomo Bank Hiroshima Branch

In addition to the heat rays and blast, the third major effect of the explosion was the huge amount of radiation. Gamma rays and neutrons emitted within one minute of the detonation inflicted a wide variety of physical damage to lives as far as 2.3 kilometers from the hypocenter. Those within 1 kilometer received intense radiation doses. Residual radiation caused many who entered the area within 100 hours of the explosion to suffer exposure to gamma rays. About 30 minutes after the bombing, heavy rain began falling in areas to the northwest of the city. It was the "black rain" that was full of dirt, dust soot and highly radioactive particles that were sucked up into the air at the time of the explosion and during the fire. Continuing raining for some 90 minutes, the "black rain" caused contamination not only to humans, but also to plants and animals in areas that were even remote from the explosion [Fig.2-19].

In total, it was estimated that 85% of the buildings in the city standing within 3 kilometers of the hypocenter were significantly damaged and over 90% of Hiroshima's buildings were burned or collapsed [Fig.2-20, Fig.2-21]. According to the City of Hiroshima, at the time of the bombing, Hiroshima was home to approximately 350,000 people, including 280,000 to 290,000 civilians (Japanese and non-Japanese), 20,000 Korean forced laborers and 43,000 soldiers. About 80,000 were killed instantly or seriously wounded. By the end of December 1945, it was estimated that 140,000 of the 350,000 had died from the bomb in the 4-month period following the explosion. Available figures from Manhattan Engineer District show that the population of the city then was 255,000, and the total casualties was believed to be 135,000, including 66,000 dead and 69,000 injured.

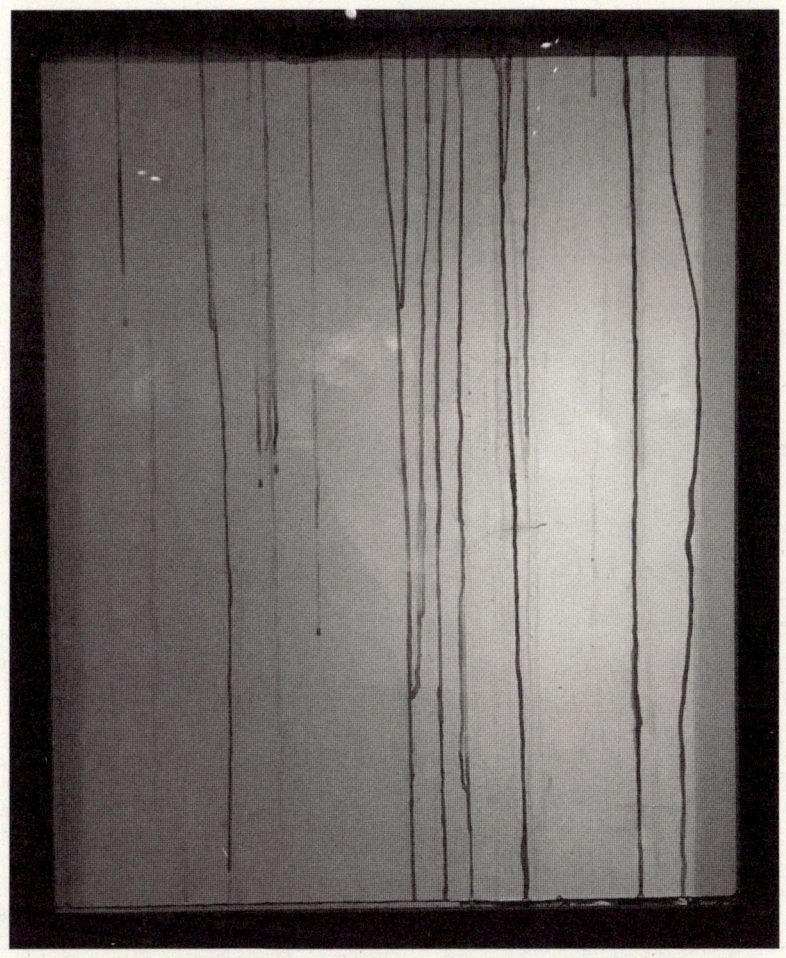

Fig.2-19 The white wall stained by black rain, displayed in the Hiroshima Peace Memorial Museum

Fig.2-20 Standing at the hypocenter in October 1945—South: People are walking on Hondori. Motoyasu River can be seen on the left in the distance. From the center to right in the distance are Ebayama Hill and Ebasarayama Hill

Fig.2-21 Standing at the hypocenter in October 1945—West: Honkawa Elementary School can be seen on the right in the distance

The Aftermath of the Hiroshima Atomic Bombing

The Atomic Bombing and Japan's Surrender

Early in the morning of 7 August 1945, American President Truman called again for Japan's surrender, warning to "expect a rain of ruin from the air, the likes of which has never been seen on this earth". Late in the evening of 8 August, the Soviet Union joined the war and took Japan's territories in Pacific and Asian-mainland. At 11:02 a.m. on 9 August, the more powerful plutonium bomb "Fat Man" was dropped by the United States on Nagasaki. Following these events, Emperor Hirohito eventually accepted the terms the Allies had set down in the Potsdam Declaration for ending the war. But agitation arose in the Army. Loyalty to the emperor was absolute in the Japanese military, but so was the refusal to surrender. Now the two had come into conflict, open rebellion became inevitable. Before the announcement of Japan's surrender, the Kyujo Incident occurred. Personnel from the Army Ministry tried to stop the move to surrender. The attempt failed, leading to some performing ritual suicide and some being arrested.

On 15 August, Emperor Hirohito gave a recorded radio announcing the unconditional surrender of Japan to the Allies, which meant a complete defeat in the Japanese War of Aggression. Public reaction toward the emperor's speech varied. Many Japanese simply listened to it then went on with their lives as usual, while several Army and Navy officers chose suicide over surrender. A few gathered in front of the Imperial Palace in Tokyo and cried, as John Dower notes in his book, the tears they shed "reflected a multitude of sentiments… anguish, regret, bereavement and anger at having been deceived, sudden emptiness and loss of purpose".

On 2 September 1945, the formal surrender took place, where representatives from the Japan Government signed the Japanese Instrument of Surrender in Tokyo Bay aboard USS Missouri [Fig.2-22]. Hereto, World War II ended with the defeat of the Axis Powers (Nazi Germany, Fascist Italy, and the Imperial Japanese) and the victory of the Anti-Fascist Allies (United State, China, United Kingdom, and Soviet Union etc.).

Fig.2-22 Japanese Foreign Minister Mamoru Shigemitsu signed the Instrument of Surrender on behalf of the Japanese Government, as General Richard K. Sutherland watched

Arguments over the Use of Atomic Bombs

Over 77 years since the U.S.'s dropping of the bombs, its use has seen a continuation of the controversy. Over the course of time, one of the primary and continuing focuses has been on the role of the bombings in Japan's surrender, which led to a quick end of the Pacific War. Most defenders assert that the bombings directly led to the Japan's surrender, thereby preventing massive casualties on both sides. While opponents argue that it was militarily unnecessary as they believe that a naval blockade and conventional bombings would have forced Japan to surrender unconditionally. Furthermore, newly developed academic accounts suggested that Japan might be more motivated to surrender by the Soviet Union's entry into the war rather than the dropping of the atomic bombs.

Regarding the ethics of the use of atomic weapons, opponents consider it as inherently immoral as using poison gas and are fully against its use particularly on a civil population. Besides, some also point to "racism" behind the use of the atomic bombs, which has long been excluded from the reasons for supporting the bombing by most defenders. Whereas defenders argue that in total war, especially as carried on in Japan, there was no difference between civilians and soldiers due to its National Mobilization Law. It seems logical that one who supports total war in principle cannot complain of war against civilians.

Overall, "Was it right?" has been the question at the heart of this matter and there is still no clear answer. But whatever forms it takes, even when it serves a just purpose, war can never be justified. Instead of searching for a right or wrong answer, it would be more helpful to gain a better understanding on the use of the atomic bombs through a collection of voices from different levels, including political and military leaders, historians, and the public.

In the speech of British Prime Minister Churchill and the letter of American President Truman, the use of atomic bombs against Japan was clearly mentioned as a quick way to end the war to save money and lives of both sides. In fact, a few days after the bombing, President Truman also justified his decision by emphasizing the unprovoked Japanese attack on Pearl Harbor and Japan's brutal murder of American prisoners. As he once wrote: "When you have to deal with a beast you have to treat him as a beast." Nevertheless, the notion that speedy ending of the war saved millions of lives is still the greatest justification among most of the supporters.

Antony Beevor, a British military historian, expressed his full understanding regarding President Truman's decision that few actions in war were morally justifiable, and all a commander or political leader could hope to assess was a particular course of action to reduce the loss of life. He further demonstrated that what America feared the most was the fact that the Imperial Japanese Army could never contemplate surrender. Japan had forced all their men to fight to the death since the start of the war. All civilians were mobilized and forced to fight with bamboo spears and satchel charges to act as suicide bombers against Allied tanks. According to Japanese documents, it apparently indicated that their army was prepared to accept up to 28 million civilian deaths.

Regarding the critics of Japan's unwillingness to surrender unconditionally, American historian Michael Kort, argued that instead of surrender, the country was preparing a defense far more formidable than the U.S. had anticipated. He explicated that the frequently argued choice was not between using an atomic bomb against Hiroshima and landing on Japan but was that there was no one on the Allied side who could say with confidence what would bring about a Japanese surrender. The bombs were used hoping to convince Tokyo to surrender, but how many would be needed was said to be an open question. After Hiroshima, the Japanese Government had three days to respond before the Nagasaki atomic bombing but it did not do so. Emperor Hirohito and some of his advisers knew Japan had to surrender but were not able to get the Government to accept that conclusion. Key military members of the Government argued that it was unlikely that the U.S. could have a second bomb and, even if it did, public pressure would prevent its use.

Among the defenders, there were also Japanese leaders who publicly supported the idea of the dropping of the bombs leading to a quick end of the war. "I now have come to understand that the bombing brought the war to its end. Though there were countless numbers of people suffering great tragedies in Nagasaki (and Hiroshima), I think it was something that couldn't be helped." This infamous "couldn't be helped" remark was made by Kyuma Fumio, the former Defense Minister, on 30 June 2007, at Reitaku University in Kashiwa, Chiba prefecture. His statements seemed to justify the U.S. atomic bomb attacks on Hiroshima and Nagasaki, and it sparked a great public outcry in Japan. Hence, the next day, the Nagasaki-native minister was made to apologize and finally on 3 July he submitted his resignation.

Although it is hard to break through the mythmaking within the U.S. mindset that atomic bombs were needed to force Japan's surrender to lead to a quick end of the war, not all historians, scientists and military men agreed to the decision. Before Little Boy was dropped on Hiroshima, Leo Szilard at Met Lab in Chicago tried to stop its use, though he was the one who had led atomic bomb research in 1939. He started a petition to President Truman against bombing Japan, and eventually collected 88 signatures. After learning of the petition, General Leslie Groves polled the Met Lab scientists, where only 15 percent wanted the bomb to be used "in the most effective military manner". However, both Szilard's petition and Groves's poll of the Met Lab scientists had somewhat been filed away, thus President Truman had never seen them.

After the war, voices claiming the bombings were either militarily unnecessary or morally reprehensible also appeared. Among them, according to American historian Gar Alperovitz, there were American five-star military officers, such as Admiral William Leahy and General Dwight Eisenhower, who stated that Japan was already defeated before the first bomb fell and the dropping of the bombs was completely unnecessary. Richard Overy, a British historian, also supported this argument, indicating that when the Soviet Union joined the war on 8 August Japan had already been militarily finished. In other words, further blockade and urban destruction would have produced a surrender in August or September at the latest and there was no need for the costly anticipated landing or the atomic bomb.

While concerning the public opinions among the Americans and Japanese, for Americans, most of them have consistently approved of the A-bomb attack and have said it was justified, while most of the Japanese have not. The 1945 Gallup poll immediately after the bombing found that 85% of Americans approved of using the new atomic weapon on Japanese cities, claiming that it saved a great number of American lives by shortening the war. But opinions are changing. The Americans are less and less supportive of their use of atomic weapons, and the Japanese are more and more opposed. In 1991, according to a Detroit Free Press survey conducted in both the U.S. and Japan, 63% of Americans said the atomic bomb attacks on Japan were justified means of ending the war, while only 29% thought the action was unjustified. Only 29% of Japanese said the bombing was justified, while 64% thought it was unwarranted.

Lately in 2015, Pew Research Center reported its new result on the same questions, claiming that only 47% of Americans aged 18 to 29 years old said the use of atomic weapons was justified, compared to 70% of those aged 65 or older. It is a good sign that young Americans' support for the use of atomic bombs was declining, but it did not mean Americans thought they had to apologize for having done so. In the same Gallup survey, 73% said the U.S. should not formally apologize to Japan for the atomic bomb attacks on Hiroshima and Nagasaki, while only 20% suggested an official apology was needed. To some extent, Obama's visit to Hiroshima in 2016, where Obama was expected only to give a speech on nonproliferation of nuclear weapons rather than to apologize for the dropping of the bombs, reflected this trend.

Chapter 3
Striving for Peace from the Grassroots

Anti-War Movement

After the war defeat, Japan was occupied by the Allied Forces. Unlike Germany that was occupied by the U.S., the U.K., France and the Soviet Union, Japan was ruled by the U.S. alone. The occupying force was called the Supreme Commander of the Allied Powers (SCAP) or known as the General Headquarters (GHQ) in Japan. As the occupation of Japan was indirect, the Japanese Government, to some extent, continued to exist and function. The initial objectives of U.S. occupation were to demilitarize and democratize Japan.

Accordingly, a new Constitution was promulgated on 3 November 1946 and came into effect on 3 May 1947. In terms of warfare, the new Constitution abandons not only the right of belligerency but also prohibits maintaining military forces. Thus, it is also widely known as the Peace Constitution. Represented in Article 9, it reads: "Aspiring sincerely to an international peace based on justice and order, the Japanese people forever renounce war as a sovereign right of the nation and the threat or use of force as means of settling international disputes. To accomplish the aim of the preceding paragraph, land, sea, and air forces, as well as other war potential, will never be maintained. The right of belligerency of the state will not be recognized." [Fig.3-1]

一 憲法改正、法律、政令及び條約を公布すること。
二 國會を召集すること。
三 衆議院を解散すること。
四 國會議員の總選擧の施行を公示すること。
五 國務大臣及び法律の定めるその他の官吏の任免並びに全權委任狀及び大使及び公使の信任狀を認證すること。
六 大赦、特赦、減刑、刑の執行の免除及び復權を認證すること。
七 榮典を授與すること。
八 批准書及び法律の定めるその他の外交文書を認證すること。
九 外國の大使及び公使を接受すること。
十 儀式を行ふこと。
第八條 皇室に財産を讓り渡し、又は皇室が、財産を讓り受け、若しくは賜與することは、國會の議決に基かなければならない。

第二章 戰爭の放棄

第九條 日本國民は、正義と秩序を基調とする國際平和を誠實に希求し、國權の發動たる戰爭と、武力による威嚇又は武力の行使は、國際紛爭を解決する手段としては、永久にこれを放棄する。
前項の目的を達するため、陸海空軍その他の戰力は、これを保持しない。國の交戰權は、これを認めない。

Fig.3-1 Article 9 of the new Constitution, 3 November 1946

Apart from renouncing war, the Constitution granted new civil and social rights to Japanese citizens since the lack of democracy was considered to be conducive to Japan's military expansion. Equally important was the legalization of the Japanese leftist in the following years. During wartime, the socialists and organized laborers were violently suppressed, as they had long been the main force of anti-war activities since the outbreak of the Sino-Japanese War of 1894-1895. In late 1945, when the workers were given the right to organize, union membership exploded. Soon, they were affiliated with and represented by Japanese socialist and communist political parties. However, the outpouring of left-wing activism was short-lived.

In 1947, the Cold War (1947-1991) started generally considered to be with the announcement of the Truman Doctrine on 12 March. U.S. occupation policy over Japan shifted dramatically. Now the U.S. wanted to strengthen Japan as its capitalist ally and an anti-communist base in East Asia, by facilitating its economic recovery and political rehabilitation. Apart from offering economic aid to Japan for its remilitarization, the U.S. also rehabilitated several notorious wartime leaders making them America's greatest supporters in Japan. Since then, remilitarization and the economic recovery of Japan, including the rebuilding of heavy industries, were promoted.

With the outbreak of the Korean War (1950-1953) in 1950, an anti-war movement organized by the leftist activists with the support of the Japanese Communist Party (JCP) started, protesting U.S. military bases in Japan as well as protecting Japan's Peace Constitution Article 9. Among the activists who tried to stop Japan from producing and sending arms to U.S. forces in the Korean peninsula, there were not only Japanese but also Koreans in Japan. Unfortunately, many of them were arrested by the Japanese police and sentenced by the U.S. occupation forces to multiple years of confinement with hard labor. In the case of leftist Koreans, they often faced additional punishment of deportation to South Korea, where a death sentence was awaited. In the end, Japan's transforming itself into a "huge supply depot" to collaborate with the U.S. during the Korean War, led to the Japanese economy entering a period of high growth.

On 8 September 1951, as a condition to end the U.S. occupation of Japan, Japan signed the Japan-U.S. Security Treaty (Anpo Treaty), allowing U.S. military forces stationed across Japan for any purpose without prior consultation with the Japanese Government. No expiration or renewal date was specified. Scandalously, the Treaty even permitted the U.S. to use its force against the Japanese, such as to put down domestic protests in Japan, but did not commit the U.S. to defending Japan if Japan was attacked by a third party. This time the focus of the anti-war movement shifted to anti-Anpo, and among protesters many were Japanese leftist while some were conservatives on the right.

During the same period, American nuclear testing, and a series of conflicts between U.S. troops and Japanese residents further widened the opposition. In facing the strong anti-U.S. sentiment among the public, President Dwight Eisenhower agreed to revise the Anpo Treaty. However, what the protesters hoped was to get rid of the treaty and the Japan-U.S. Alliance entirely. Together with the increasing Cold War tensions, the anti-Anpo movement continued to grow larger. Over the end of 1959 and into 1960, the movement was supported by numerous organizations that include not only socialists, communists, labor union members, anti-nuclear and anti-base activists, but also student groups and women's societies, prominent intellectuals, and artists.

Ultimately, the 1960 anti-Anpo movement did not achieve its goal to stop the revised Anpo Treaty [Fig.3-2] from taking effect. But the strong anti-U.S. sentiment changed the incoming administration of President Kennedy's approach to the Japan-U.S. relations, where the U.S. promised to treat Japan more likely as a close ally, especially in supporting Japan's economic growth. Around the 1970s, when the Vietnam War (1961-1975) broke out, a few student groups, civic groups and the anti-Vietnam War organizations again held a series of protests against the Anpo Treaty, but little attention was paid as the focus of the movement during that time had largely shifted to anti-nuclear weapons.

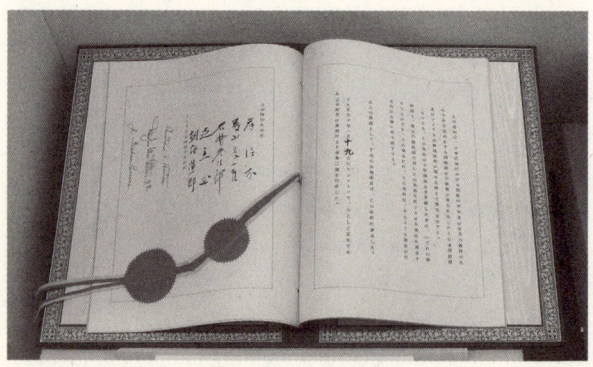

Fig.3-2 The revised Anpo Treaty in 1960

Anti-Nuclear Weapons Movement

Japan's unique experience of the Hiroshima and Nagasaki atomic bombings gave the Japanese an exclusive claim to leadership of the world Anti-Nuclear Weapons Movement. But along with peace education, the mainstream of the earliest peace movement did not address the nuclear issues, largely due to GHQ's restriction. On 19 March 1950, the Stockholm Appeal was launched by the World Peace Council in Stockholm, Sweden, promoting nuclear disarmament and preventing nuclear war. The Appeal declared that any government that was the first to use atomic weapons was committing a crime against humanity and called on people to sign the declaration. A worldwide signature campaign followed. Japan also launched its first widespread campaign against atomic weapons. Led by the Japan Committee for Maintaining Peace (JCMP; Heiwa Yogo Hihon Iinkai), the petition eventually collected 6.45 million signatures in Japan thanks to the people power. However, it was during the period of the Red Purge, where anything remotely associated with communism was suspected. As a result, the Stockholm Appeal was denounced as a "Red Movement" and its impact was extremely limited. But people power did not fade away.

Ban-the-Bomb Movement

By the end of the occupation in 1951, the Japanese media finally brought forward the extraordinary destruction and lingering suffering caused by the atomic bombs. But at the time, it was often seen as a regional story with no special significance for the nation. Not until the infamous 1954 Lucky Dragon Incident (also known as Bikini Incident), did nuclear issues attract nationwide attention in Japan. On 1 March, the Japanese tuna fishing boat Daigo Fukuryu Maru, with a crew of 23 fishmen, was exposed to nuclear fallout from a U.S. hydrogen bomb test at the Bikini Atoll in the Pacific Ocean [Fig.3-3]. Many of the crew members began to develop symptoms of radiation poisoning as early as the evening after exposure.

Fig.3-3 The bow of Daigo Fukuryu Maru displayed in Daigo Fukuryu Maru Exhibition Hall, 1 July 2007

Concerning the incident, the Japanese Government made a quick response the day after it happened. Except for the purchasing of the contaminated boat, the Government also provided medical treatment and immediate financial compensation to the crew members. Despite receiving medical treatment, Aikichi Kuboyama, 40-year-old chief radioman of the boat died from radiation sickness on 23 September 1954. The loss of this crew member made it even clearer how dangerous the radiation damage could bring to life and the popular fears towards nuclear bombs reached a peak. The incident was also recognized by the Japanese as its third time being victimized by nuclear energy.

Due to the incident, the fish market was temporarily closed and fishmongers as well as sushi dealers soon lost their business. In response to the crisis, they gathered at the auditorium in Tsukiji Market in Tokyo and launched a campaign to collect signatures against atomic and hydrogen bombs and gain compensation for the losses they had. But the first to formally protest for the crew members' exposure to radioactive fallout was the city assembly of the Daigo Fukuryu Maru's home port, Yaizu. Quickly, it was followed by the National Diet in early April and then by the other assemblies.

In mid-April, the Suginami Ward Assembly in Tokyo passed its resolution against the hydrogen bomb and a special council was founded to deal with the petition movement on 9 May. By the end of June, the Suginami Appeal had gathered some 270,000 signatures, suggesting almost all the adult population in Suginami had signed. In achieving such a success, middle-class women, especially housewives played a key role in circulating the petition nationwide. With the fear of radiation poisoning infecting the whole nation, the appeal attracted wide attention and finally on 8 August a National Council for a Petition Movement to Ban Atomic and Hydrogen Bombs (hereafter, the National Council) was found. After the death of the crew member of the Daigo Fukuryu Maru in September, the petition movement surged and eventually resulted in 32.59 million signatures by August 1955.

To maintain momentum, the National Council decided to inaugurate annual Ban-the-Bomb conventions beginning in 1955. On 6 August 1955, the first World Conference against Atomic and Hydrogen Bombs took place at the Municipal Auditorium (now the Hiroshima International Conference Center), located in Hiroshima Peace Memorial Park. In the first World Conference, the Japan Council against Atomic and Hydrogen Bombs (Gensuikyo, supported by the Japanese Communist Party) was established to continue the petition movement and promote assistance to the survivors of the Hiroshima and Nagasaki atomic bombings.

During the mid-1970s, the campaign was divided into two groups due to conflict over the group's stance on nuclear tests conducted by the Soviet Union, with the other organization called the Japan Congress against Atomic and Hydrogen Bombs (Gensuikin, supported by the Japan Socialist Party). Thereafter, Gensuikyo and Gensuikin separately held their own world conferences, inviting peace groups and researchers from the globe to Hiroshima and Nagasaki discussing ways to realize the elimination of nuclear weapons. Being the two main arms of the grassroots-based Anti-Nuclear Weapons Movement, Gensuikyo and Gensuikin joined together around 1977, but since 1986 they have once again become separate bodies.

As the call for abolishing nuclear weapons grew louder, more civil society organizations, national and international, joined this massive movement against nuclear weapons. Mayors for Peace is one good model worth introducing. As an international organization of cities dedicated to the promotion of peace, it was established in 1982 at the initiative of then Mayor of Hiroshima Takeshi Araki. Its major purpose is to contribute to the attainment of lasting world peace by arousing concerns among citizens of the world for the total abolition of nuclear weapons through close solidarity among member cities [Fig.3-4]. Launched in Hiroshima and Nagasaki, as of July 2022, Mayors for Peace is having 8,188 member cities of 166 countries and regions joined the network, supporting the commencement of negotiations towards the elimination of nuclear weapons.

In addition to collaborating with member cities, Mayors for Peace also forges partnerships with citizen groups, NGOs, and other organizations around the world. One of its linked partner organizations is the 2017 Nobel Peace Prize winner—The International Campaign to Abolish Nuclear Weapons (ICAN). Formally launched in April 2007, ICAN is a global civil society coalition of 570 non-governmental organizations in 105 countries, seeking to promote adherence to and full implementation of the Treaty on the Prohibition of Nuclear Weapons (TPNW).

Fig.3-4 A stone slab in the Peace Memorial Park, erected in Japanese: an end to nuclear weapons on the earth

To draw attention to the catastrophic anti-humanitarian consequences of any use of nuclear weapons and to achieve a treaty-based prohibition of nuclear weapons, ICAN served as the civil society coordinator for each of the Review Conference of the Treaty on the Non-Proliferation of Nuclear Weapons (NPT), bringing together most of the world's governments, along with international organizations and academic institutions. Building on the outcomes of the humanitarian conferences, ICAN campaigned for the establishment of a treaty to prohibit nuclear weapons at the UN. In achieving this strongest and most effective treaty, ICAN, being the main civil society actor, worked tirelessly alongside governments throughout the negotiating process. Eventually on 7 July 2017, TPNW was officially adopted and on 22 January 2021, the treaty entered into force.

A-bomb Survivors Aid Movement

Along with the development of the Anti-Nuclear Weapons Movement, the voices of A-bomb survivors (also known as hibakusha) have played a fundamental role in spreading the messages of nuclear disarmament worldwide. But before they were brought to light, their fight for support, financial and medical, already started. As subjects of scientific research, A-bomb survivors were initially provided with assistance under the Wartime Casualties Care Law of 1942. However, the National Government stopped being supportive as soon as the Law's validity expired in early October 1945. Since many survivors were desperately in need of medical care, Hiroshima prefecture designated six hospitals in the city to provide care for them. But since they were suffering in a very different way from the other war victims, local hospitals that were short of capable doctors and nurses were paralyzed by many new symptoms developed by survivors.

Soon after the attack of Hiroshima, A-bomb damage investigations were carried out by several U.S. teams, gathering essential data concerning the destructive power of atomic bombing. Whereas most of the results were unable to be published because of the press code ordered by the GHQ, on 19 September 1945, to control newspapers and other publications in Japan. Even so, the public still had limited access to A-bomb related materials. Thanks to that small amount of information, A-bomb survivors began to organize themselves, demanding special assistance from the National Government in the early 1950s.

Followed by the enforcement of the San Francisco Peace Treaty in April 1952, the press code was eventually phased out. Subsequently, A-bomb related information became widely published, which raised the awareness of the aftereffects of the bombing. As the awareness grew rapidly, the number of A-bomb survivors was on a dramatic increase. In January 1953, the Hiroshima City Atomic Bomb Casualty Treatment Council (Gentaikyo) was established, aiming to "investigate and promote research and treatment measures on injuries due to the atomic bombing". But due to the lack of funds, investigation and medical treatment remained in a critical situation.

In 1954, the Lucky Dragon Incident occurred, and the National Government promptly offered proper treatment for the crew members. Having been suffering from similar symptoms, A-bomb survivors had not yet received such treatment from the National Government. Thus, this very different reaction triggered dissatisfaction from Hiroshima and Nagasaki. Following the nationwide grassroots Anti-Nuclear Weapons Movement calling for the prohibition of atomic and hydrogen tests provoked by the Incident, the voices of A-bomb survivors were gradually brought to light. Consequently, the sufferings of Hiroshima and Nagasaki came to be acknowledged as "the sufferings of Japan". In the meantime, a strong anti-U.S. sentiment nationwide was ignited, especially when the Japan-U.S. Security Alliance allowed the U.S. to continue its military presence even though the occupation was ended.

Being challenged by the civilian protest, both pro-nuclear governments—Japan and the U.S. were pushed to make their informed choices. Considering that the Japanese Government had started their plans on developing atomic energy before the Lucky Dragon Incident, the U.S. decided to assist Japan in organizing a campaign for the "peaceful use" of atomic energy, aiming to calm down the anti-nuclear sentiment as well

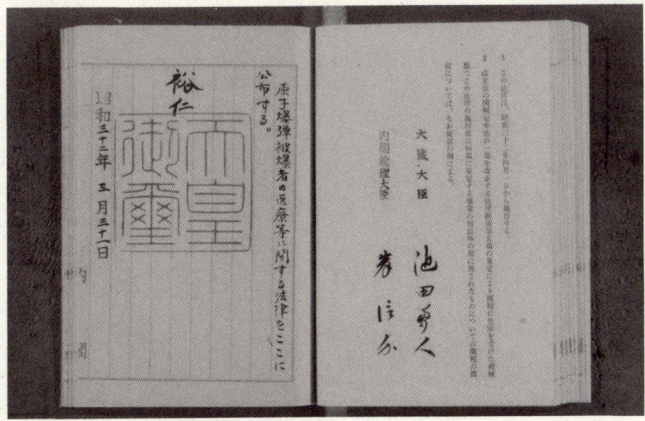

Fig.3-5 Front page of the 1957 Medical Law

as the anti-U.S. nationalism in Japan. Gaining support from the U.S., the Japanese Government took a significant step forward in its development of atomic energy. Meanwhile, the Government also began to prepare protective measures from radioactive materials to calm the public, which ironically helped to legitimize A-bomb survivors' demand for medical assistance from the state.

In other words, the Lucky Dragon Incident and the government-initiated program for the utilization of atomic energy paved the way toward the law-making process to offer aid to A-bomb survivors. Eventually in March 1957, Atomic Bomb Survivors Medical Care Law (hereafter, the 1957 Medical Law) was established [Fig.3-5]. But it aimed to provide medical relief for survivors who had only been suffering from health damage caused by radiation from the atomic bombing within a certain distance from the hypocenter of the explosion at the time of bombing.

Due to the strict limitation of the subject, only a few survivors were eligible to receive aid under the 1957 Medical Law. Hence, in the following years, several "atomic bomb lawsuits" were filed by survivors demanding national compensation, recognition of atomic bomb syndrome, recognition as hibakusha and refinements to the legal system of compensation. Those efforts from the grassroots paid off and made the 1957 Medical Law undergo multiple amendments, which led to the implementation of Atomic Bomb Survivors Special Law (hereafter, the 1968 Special Law). Thereafter, special allowance and other measures began to be offered to A-bomb survivors.

Nevertheless, the movement protesting to win support for A-bomb survivors went on, because there were a certain number of victims from other nations, among whom Koreans occupied the largest percentage with its number reaching 25,000 to 28,000. One estimated that the number of Chinese who experienced the Hiroshima atomic bombing was several dozen to several hundred, among them between 20 and 240 were killed. The rest of non-Japanese victims also include 3,200 Japanese Americans, a dozen American prisoners of war, 8 foreign students from Southeast Asia, 7 Russians and 2 Germans. In 1974, the Ministry of Health, Labor, and Welfare (MHLW) issued a directive, stipulating that A-bomb survivors who were outside Japan would not be eligible for relief measures as well as any allowances.

Such a gap in relief measures between survivors in Japan and survivors overseas provoked more "atomic bomb lawsuits". Thankfully in 1978, the oversea A-bomb survivors were eligible to apply for the A-bomb survivor certificate (a medical notebook to represent their special identity). Yet, many were unable to visit Japan in person to go through the overall procedure to receive the medical notebook, due to poor health and financial conditions. Followed by several lawsuits in 2002, special financial aid to cover most of the transportation fees for survivors to visit

Japan started. And eventually in 2008, applications without visiting Japan in person became available. In short, without the persistent efforts paid by A-bomb survivors and many civil society organizations, all these transformative results would not have been possible.

After examining the development of Ban-the-Bomb Movement and A-bomb Survivors Aid Movement, the Lucky Dragon Incident played a key role in provoking the storm of protesting against the nuclear weapons. But why was it not the Hiroshima atomic bombing? It is understandable that the Lucky Dragon Incident is more likely to raise the popular fear of radiation poisoning affecting the whole nation, since fish has long been the center of Japanese food culture. But if we were to compare the number of deaths (though it is incomparable at all), it is difficult to believe that it was the Lucky Dragon Incident rather than the Hiroshima atomic bombing that paved the way for the Anti-Nuclear Weapons Movement and the law-making process for aid providing to survivors.

As it has been emphasized many times, before the end of the U.S. occupation, strict censorship had prevented information on the destruction of atomic bombing from being known to the public, which belated the Anti-Nuclear Weapons Movement. But the sharply opposite reactions from both the Japanese Government and U.S. Government towards the two events are still puzzling. Apart from the overwhelming civilian protest and anti-U.S. sentiment, another reason that triggered such a huge difference could be that unlike the Hiroshima atomic bombing, the Lucky Dragon Incident has nothing to do with war. Specifically, if it was to relate to the war, Japan's past aggression before Hiroshima was bombed and the controversial act of the U.S.'s dropping of the atomic bomb on Hiroshima would be unavoidably reminded of. However, the fact is that both Japan and the U.S. share an ideology of "starting over", which is largely based on a deliberate amnesia to escape from their troubled history.

Peace Movement

Slightly distinct from the Anti-War Movement and Anti-Nuclear Weapons Movement introduced previously, there is a stream of force among the movement that seeks to spread peace in a more comprehensive manner, encompassing both messages of no more war and no more nuclear weapons. The A-bombed Sites Preservation Movement and the Peace Movement led by artists are good examples to look at.

A-bombed Sites Preservation Movement

The A-bombed Sites Preservation Movement aims to preserve A-bombed sites including trees and buildings that also experienced and witnessed Hiroshima's transformation from a military city to a city of peace. As the A-bomb survivors are aging, and many have already passed away, the precious opportunities to listen to their first-hand stories are becoming fewer. Unlike survivors, trees and buildings, with proper renovation and protection, can serve as permanent testaments to the destructive power of war and nuclear weapons, which makes the preservation work more significant.

A-bombed Trees Protection

After the atomic bombing of Hiroshima, with landscapes demolished, soils charred and radiation rampant, it was once estimated that Hiroshima would be barren of life, and nothing would grow for 75 years. But the following spring, to everyone's surprise and delight, new shoots were seen springing up among the debris of the city. First bloomed the oleander flowers and sprouted the Chinese parasol trees, which brought a tremendous amount of courage and hope to people in Hiroshima. For its remarkable powers of regeneration, in 1973, the oleander was designated the official flower of Hiroshima city. Being the earliest A-bombed tree that had new buds in the spring of 1946, the Chinese parasol tree is now a symbol of peace. Its seeds have been spread around the world to express the genuine wish of Hiroshima for a nuclear-free planet.

Today, hundreds of trees that are standing in the city were around the vicinity where the bomb dropped. Although broken and heavily charred, they survived and soon were healthy again. As the living witness to the tragic history of the atomic bombing, their strong vitality beautifully demonstrates the important message: War brings death, but life brings peace. To ensure that every living being enjoys a loving life, peaceful means must be invented and advocated to replace war or any form of violence. Having been officially registered as A-bombed trees or hibaku trees, each of them is now identified by an introductory plaque.

In collecting and sharing stories of A-bombed trees, Green Legacy Hiroshima (GLH) plays a significant role. Supported by UNITAR and a Hiroshima-based non-governmental organization named Asian Network of Hiroshima (ANT-Hiroshima), the global volunteer initiative GLH was established in 2011. With assistance from a group of volunteers and translators, GLH and ANT-Hiroshima created a "Database of A-bombed Trees of Hiroshima" in English. It includes detailed descriptions and photos of 170 A-bombed trees in 55 locations within a radius of approximately 2,000 meters from the hypocenter [Fig.3-6 to Fig.3-10].

Actively collaborating with institutions, such as Mayors for Peace, the Hiroshima Peace Cultural Foundation and Hiroshima University, GLH also helps to spread peace messages with seeds and seedlings of the A-bombed trees worldwide. Wishing that trees would be properly cared for, GHL first built connections with universities, botanical gardens and other public institutions that have basic knowledge and experience in planting, and later moved on to city parks, schools, and other public facilities. Further efforts were made to plant trees at or near the former nuclear test sites in the United States and the Soviet Union, where there are radiation victims suffering as much as survivors of Hiroshima and Nagasaki. As of 2022, seeds and seedlings of the A-bombed trees have been sent to and are growing in 35 countries.

Fig.3-6 The kurogane holly near the Shirakami Shrine, 530 meters from the hypocenter. According to the plaque, the aboveground part was completely burned out, leaving only the stump. As sprouts grew from the left-over stump, the tree came into its today's form

Fig.3-7 The eucalyptus tree at Hiroshima Castle. Located 740 meters from the hypocenter, this tree survived the bombing, while the castle was destroyed

Fig.3-8 The A-bombed Chinese parasol trees in the Hiroshima Peace Memorial Park. Being the earliest A-bombed trees sprouted and showed the greatest power of survival, Chinese parasol trees are especially appreciated by Hiroshima citizens. A song called "Aogiri no Uta" was created by a 9-year-old girl, to express her gratitude towards the trees, and it can be listened to with the audio system in front of the tree

Fig.3-9 The giant pussy willow near the entrance of Hiroshima Castle

Fig.3-10 The large ginkgo tree (estimated to be planted in 1850) at Hosenbo Temple. Exploded at about 1,130 meters away from the hypocenter, the ginkgo survived the bombing while the temple was destroyed. Later, the main building of the temple was rebuilt having its stairs in front divided into left- and right-hand sides, protecting the ginkgo inside the U-shape

A-bombed Buildings Preservation

Unlike the A-bombed trees that brought life and hope to the survivors soon after the bombing, A-bombed buildings were treated very differently, considering they were the reminders of the horror that could cause re-traumatization. Therefore, many favored removing every physical remnant of the tragedy to rebuild Hiroshima into a completely new city for peace. Today, only a few A-bombed buildings are still standing in the city, thanks to the efforts paid by A-bomb survivors and civilian groups who believe the historical value of A-bombed buildings speaks louder than any words to call for lasting peace.

The most well-known A-bombed building is the A-bomb Dome (for details please refer to Chapter 4). In December 1996, the Dome was designated a World Heritage Site, which guaranteed some of the other A-bombed buildings be preserved too [Fig.3-11].

Fig.3-11 A-bomb Dome

Fig.3-12 The Rest House of Hiroshima Peace Memorial Park after renewal in 2020

Rest House [Fig.3-12], the previous modern-looking Kimono Shop that was located at the opposite side of the Hiroshima Prefectural Industrial Promotion Hall (today's A-bomb Dome), is one good example. Due to the attack, its roof and portions of the walls were severely damaged, but the building avoided collapse. After being renovated several times, it now serves as the hub for tourist information with its basement preserved as it was on 6 August 1945 to show the scars of the atomic bombing [Fig.3-13].

Fig.3-13 The basement of the Rest House

Several other A-bombed buildings share similar experiences like the Rest House. The former Bank of Japan Hiroshima Branch, the only structure on Rijo-dori Avenue that retains its appearance, is now open to the public and used by civic groups for cultural and peace activities [Fig.3-14, Fig.3-15]. The former Honkawa Elementary School, the closest school to the hypocenter, with its basement and part of the original A-bombed school building preserved as a testament to the destructive power of nuclear weapons, today serves as a peace museum displaying exhibits collected from A-bombed sites [Fig.3-16]. The Former Fukuromachi Elementary School, which was almost demolished due to deterioration, was able to be reformed as a peace museum because of the left messages found written on its black burned walls by survivors. Currently, it is also exhibiting precious A-bombed materials that have remained to date, especially the messages left behind (hibaku dengon).

Fig.3-14 Former Bank of Japan Hiroshima Branch around November 1945

Fig.3-15 Former Bank of Japan Hiroshima Branch—the only A-bombed structure on Rijo-dori Avenue that retains its appearance

Fig.3-16 Honkawa Elementary School Peace Museum

The most recent A-bombed Sites Preservation Campaign carried out in 2019 was to preserve the Former Hiroshima Army Clothing Depot (or Former Deshio Army Uniform Depot) [Fig.3-17]. Built in 1913, it was one of the largest buildings left standing after the A-bomb attack. Back then, all the four buildings served as a facility responsible for the production, repair, storage, and delivery of military outfit items, such as clothes, hats, and accessories worn by Japanese soldiers of the notorious Hiroshima-based Fifth Division. Today, three of the four buildings are owned by Hiroshima prefecture, and the rest one is state-owned property. However, as the buildings are not earthquake-resistant and will cost a fortune for its reinforcement work, in December 2019, Hiroshima prefecture announced a plan to demolish two of the prefecture-owned buildings by 2022.

Regarding the demolition proposal, the City of Hiroshima expressed the understanding about the need for safety and financial concerns but insisted that the entire buildings should be preserved as much as possible. Together with the city, calls from Hiroshima residents also showed their strong willingness to preserve all three buildings. To gather more attention, an online petition was organized by civilians calling on the prefectural government to preserve the depot. Till December 2019, it was estimated more than 15,000 signatures had been collected. As a result, in May 2021 the prefecture revealed its willingness to preserve all buildings and decided to go ahead with reinforcement work, but official plans are yet to be confirmed. Many civilian supporters hope to use the buildings as a historical and educational center for the public, citing their greatest historical value to tell the lessons from past war and send the message of peace.

Fig.3-17 Former Hiroshima Army Clothing Depot (deformed iron windows reveal the power of the blast)

Peace Movement by Artists

Art has long been seen as a powerful and creative tool to promote peace. Among the peace movements, there were always the artists. As a special civic force, they contributed their poetry, novels, and visual images to sharpening the horror of the atomic bombings and evoking the human dimension of these catastrophic events. All these artworks are great resources for peace education and peace movement, spreading the genuine peace message of no more war and no more nuclear weapons worldwide.

Despite the strict censorship, beginning in the spring of 1946, poets, professional or amateur, in Hiroshima quickly responded to the horror through their works. They first started with the most traditional forms like haiku and tanka, however since the atomic horror was beyond the possibilities of such verses to express, free verse became more frequently used. Gradually, the unique genre of atomic bomb literature (hibaku bungaku) came into being, which played a key role in helping the public understand the destructiveness of the arms that humankind ever created as well as the importance of ultimate elimination of nuclear weapons.

"In Hiroshima, it was the poets who most quickly responded to the atomic bombing through their works," said Munetoshi Fukagawa (1921-2008), a poet himself who survived the Hiroshima atomic bombing. Indeed, the poetry served as a kind of authentic "evidence" and recording of the horror of the atomic bombing. Belonging to the group of poets who witnessed the bombing themselves and wrote about it in detail, there were Sadako Kurihara, Tamiki Hara, Yoko Ota, Toge Sankichi and many more. Among them, Sadako Kurihara was the first to publish her major collection of poems, *Black Eggs*, also the very first book of atomic bomb literature in 1946. Being highly censored and republished in 1986 in a restored uncensored format, *Black Eggs* provided a unique insight into the A-bomb and its effect on humankind. For example, one of her most widely quoted poems is "Let Us Be Midwives!" (Umashimen ka na), which focuses on the optimistic side of humanity in the center of atrocity, trying to wake up those who has completely become machines due to dehumanizing logic in the wartime.

Let Us Be Midwives!
> —*An untold story of the atomic bombing*

Night in the basement of a concrete structure now in ruins.
Victims of the atomic bomb
jammed the room;
it was dark—not even a single candle.
The smell of fresh blood, the stench of death,
the closeness of sweaty people, the moans—
From out of all that, lo and behold, a voice:
"The baby's coming!"
In that hellish basement, at that very moment,
a young woman had gone into labor,
In the dark, without a single match, what to do?
People forgot their own pains, worried about her
And then:"I'm a midwife; I'll help with the birth."
The speaker, seriously injured herself,
had been moaning only moments before.
And so new life was born in the dark of that pit of hell.
And so the midwife died before dawn, still bathed in blood,
Let us be midwives!
Let us be midwives!
Even if we lay down our own lives to do so.

(translated by Richard Minear)

Like Kurihara, the intolerable experience of the atomic bombing also changed the life of Tamiki Hara and became one primary theme of his writing. *Summer Flowers* (*Natsu no Hana*) was his most important work that was based on the notes put down when he was escaping from the devastation. Thus, it has been regarded as one of the most valuable, real-time records depicting the horror immediately after the bombing. As one of the founders of atomic bomb literature, Hara was good at emphasizing the cruelty of the bombing through depicting how inhumane a human being could be after the horror. Unfortunately, he was very short-lived as he committed suicide by lying down on the busy railroad, in fear of the nuclear weapons would be used once again during the Korean War.

Another group of atomic bomb literature are the authors who didn't witness the dropping of the atomic bombs themselves but created their works based on data and interview material from victims of the atomic bombs, for example Masuji Ibuse's *Black Rain* (*Kuroi Ame*) and Oe Kenzaburo's *Hiroshima Notes* (*Hiroshima Noto*). In *Balck Rain*, Ibuse embedded the hibakusha experience within the context of more commonly experienced war suffering, which made it easier for non-hibakusha to relate to Hiroshima and incorporate it into their own stories of war victimhood [Fig.3-18]. While Oe Kenzaburo, as one of the most prominent spokesmen for atomic bomb literature, his *Hiroshima Notes* is more rational, covering a large scope of detailed truth about the miserable lives the survivors led and how radiation from the atomic bombing was still causing pain and suffering in Hiroshima in 1960s.

Fig.3-18 *Black Rain* in its English (left) and Japanese (right) versions

Apart from atomic bomb literature, visual arts also contributed a lot in spreading the horror of the Hiroshima atomic bombing worldwide. The widely known artists are painters Iri Maruki and Toshi Maruki, for their *Hiroshima Panels* (*Hiroshima no Zu*) composed of 15 paintings [Fig.3-19]; cartoonist Kenji Nakazawa, for his manga series named *Barefoot Gen* (*Hadashi no Gen*); documentary filmmaker Steven Okazaki, for several of his films documenting stories of A-bomb survivors; and photojournalist Kikujiro Fukushima, for his photo book entitled *Big Sudden Flash: The Record of an Atomic Bomb Survivor* (*Pikadon: Aru Genbaku Hisaisha no Kiroku*, hereinafter referred to as *Pikadon*).

The Marukis' *Hiroshima Panels* were recorded to be one of the first works of art in the world to resist the coming of the nuclear era. Experiencing the massive destruction in the immediate aftermath of the atomic bombing of Hiroshima, the husband-and-wife team began their collaboration on the *Hiroshima Panels* around 1948. Under the strict U.S. censorship during the occupation, the panels played a crucial role in making known the hidden nuclear sufferings across the nation. In total, there were 15 paintings, most of which were about the suffering that the atomic bombings brought to people in Hiroshima and Nagasaki, including Japanese civilians, Korean forced laborers, and American prisoners of war, etc.

Beginning in 1950, the Marukis traveled and exhibited their nuclear works in a variety of temporary settings across Japan, such as civic centers, temples, and school gymnasiums, etc. In April 1952, when the San Francisco Peace Treaty came into force ending the occupation of Japan, the first catalogue of the *Hiroshima Panels* was published by Aoki Shoten. In January the following year, the Marukis were awarded the International Peace Prize by the World Peace Council, and in June their *Hiroshima Panels* started a ten-year world tour of about 20 countries, in East Asia and Europe. In May 1967, the Marukis established their own museum to house the *Hiroshima Panels*, but the exhibition tour continued domestically and internationally.

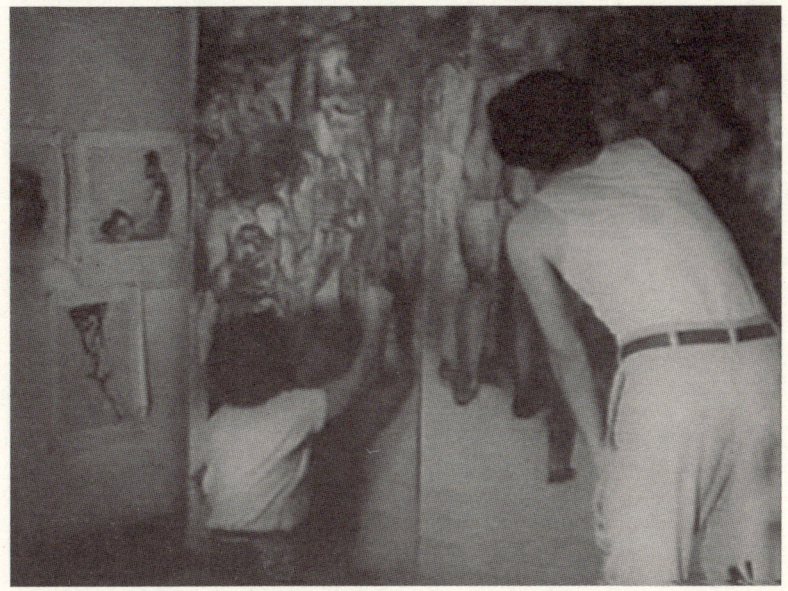

Fig.3-19 The Marukis were working on one of the *Hiroshima Panels*

Over the years, their concern over mankind's cruelty has led them to create artworks not just dealing with the Hiroshima and Nagasaki atomic bombings, but more broadly among other horrors, such as the Nanjing Massacre, Auschwitz, the Battle of Okinawa and the Minamata Mercury-Poisoning Disaster. Today, most of their works are preserved and exhibited at the Maruki Gallery, in a remote area of Saitama prefecture (near Tokyo). The Gallery offers peace education for school groups and resources for academic research on non-nuclear art and the social role of art, with the hope to capture visitors' imagination and contribute to the prevention of any war atrocities.

Different from the *Hiroshima Panels* that was a mixing of Iri's Chinese-ink-and-paper style and Toshi's Western oil-painting and portrait traditions, Keiji Nakazawa used manga—another format of narrating that originated from Japan and is popular among people of all ages and walks of life—to tell the Hiroshima story through Barefoot Gen. It is regarded as the semi-autobiographical of Keiji Nakazawa, who experienced the Hiroshima atomic bombing that led to the loss of four of his family members, including his father, two sisters and a little brother. Whereas, after several years' suffering from the atomic bomb illness, Nakazawa's mother passed away in 1966.

The death of his mother brought back the unwanted memories of the Hiroshima atomic bombing to Nakazawa. Thereafter, he started to tell his stories, which eventually led to the creation of *Barefoot Gen* [Fig.3-20]. The name of the young protagonist Gen has several meanings in Japanese, including the meaning of "root" or "origin", but also "elemental" in the sense of an atomic element as well as a "source" of vitality and happiness. Envisioning Gen as barefoot, standing firmly atop the burnt-out rubble of Hiroshima, Nakazawa tried to raise his voice against war and nuclear weapons through Gen. Meanwhile, Nakazawa also wished to convey to his readers the preciousness of peace and the courage we need to live strongly yet peacefully like the wheat depicted in the story.

Fig.3-20 The first volume of *Barefoot Gen* in its Japanese (left) and English (right) versions

Inspired by Nakazawa's work of *Barefoot Gen*, Steven Okazaki, the American documentary filmmaker, also a three-time Oscar nominee for his documentary work, became interested in Hiroshima and Nagasaki around 1980. In 1982, Okazaki conducted his first documentary work on A-bomb survivors. Entitled *Survivors*, the film features a remarkable tale of a group of twenty A-bomb survivors who either returned to or emigrated to the United States where they continue to face a range of physical, psychological, and social problems.

Hoping to increase awareness of the 1945 attacks, particularly the stories of A-bomb survivors, Okazaki created another two related films in 2005 *The Mushroom Club* and in 2007 *White Light/Black Rain: The Destruction of Hiroshima and Nagasaki*. His second documentary *The Mushroom Club* features 30 A-bomb survivors as well as several American scientists and plane navigators who were involved in the Hiroshima and Nagasaki atomic bombings. In arranging this way, Okazaki tried to tell the stories through the ordinary Japanese and American point of view with academic or political analysis. In the third film, interviews with 14 Japanese A-bomb survivors, most of whom had never spoken publicly before, and four Americans who were intimately involved in the 1945 atomic bombings of Hiroshima and Nagasaki are featured. All three works reveal the destructive power of the atomic bombs, the inconceivable human sufferings and extraordinary human resilience.

In fact, Kikujiro Fukushima, a veteran photojournalist, was the first to depict the on-going plight that A-bomb survivors faced in their daily life following the atomic horror through his lens. In his photo book *Pikadon*, Fukushima documented the A-bomb victims of Hiroshima, especially the damages done to their bodies by radiation. The book's central figure is Sugimatsu Nakamura, a man in bad health and in extreme poverty with his six children. Granted with Nakamura's permission, Fukushima documented Nakamura's anguished life and the gradual breakdown of the family. Over eight years from 1953 to 1960, Fukushima followed Nakamura everywhere and captured Nakamura's every movement, even including the moment when Nakamura was in tears on the tatami as he struggled with great pain.

However, Nakamura was only one very common figure, and his suffering compounded by poverty was shared by many A-bomb survivors in early post-war Japan. In Hiroshima, the period between 1945 and 1955 is often described as the "Blank Decade". There was little information about the lives of hibakusha and their struggles in the devastating post-war economic and social conditions. As a result, Kikujiro's early work in the 1950s and 1960s has immense historical value. His work on the life of Nakamura plays a key role in providing a visual record on the plight of many hibakusha in post-war Japan, which was what Nakamura hoped to let people throughout the world know—how painful the life of A-bomb survivors was.

Tracing back the history of various movements striving for peace, it is evident that people power from the grassroots level has played a fundamental role. Like the A-bombed trees that are miraculously able to survive and flourish despite being severely destroyed during the atomic bombing, the power united from the deep grassroots has the greatly creative potential to lead the world towards a peaceful and harmonious path that can only be achieved by nonviolence.

Chapter 4
Building up a City of Peace

After the A-bomb attack, the whole city was seriously ruined. People were struggling to comprehend the horror visited on their homes, businesses, public buildings, and fellow citizens. Although the conditions were unbelievably harsh, it was said Hiroshima's resurrection began immediately after the attack.

The day after the bombing, Genshin Takano, then governor of Hiroshima prefecture issued an official letter saying: "The damage is huge but that is the nature of war. War never stops, even for a day. We shall not stop fighting. Instead, we shall take revenge and destroy the arrogant enemy of ours." This statement perfectly reflected the Japanese national slogan of "want nothing until we win", which was implemented as part of "spiritual mobilization". The slogan was also interpreted by the U.S. that Japan would never surrender, which has become one of the justifications for the dropping of the atomic bombs. In response to Takano's declaration, Hiroshima Security Headquarters was established on the same day with a major aim to restore the city's military capability, among which communication and postal functions were of the highest priority. In rapid sequence, the restoration work on major thoroughfares, railways, streetcars, electric power, and water pumps instantly began too.

Along with the restoration of Hiroshima, relief work by the army (the Akatsuki Unit) was also carried out. Takano ordered his subordinates to rescue the wounded and provided canned food to approximately 200,000 citizens. In the first four or five days, they put forth the greatest possible effort to remove countless dead bodies, clear the main roads for truck traffic, and assist to house and treat the wounded. Urgent demand for housing turned the area near the hypocenter into a shantytown of 10,000 homes, with sanitary facilities shared among several households. Meanwhile, Higashi Police Station, being inside the 2-kilometer radius, was commandeered by the prefectural government and turned into the nerve center for search, rescue, and relief operations.

On 15 August 1945, Japan's surrender ended the war, leading to the disintegration of the military. Hence, the main force for restoration disappeared and the work was suspended. As for the city government, then Mayor Sankichi Awaya, together with approximately 920 governmental employees were among the dead. Having the city without a leader and just 80 reported for duty the following day, the local government was not capable of taking over the restoration work. Consequently, all work heavily depended on the assistance offered by many volunteers from neighboring towns and cities such as Fuchu, Kure, and even Yamaguchi. Without external help and support, Hiroshima city might not have been able to continue its journey toward recovery.

As Hiroshima was still undergoing the unforgiving force of nuclear fission, nature compounded the city's misery. Beginning late at night on 17 September and continuing through the next day, the unusually powerful Makurazaki Typhoon raged over a large area of the scorched plain, leaving the entire city under severe flood damage. Many of the temporary facilities set up on the outskirts were ruined, and bridges that survived the bombing were washed away. Railroad tracks, roads under reconstruction as well as those surviving buildings were all drenched. Some people were killed by landslides and many just disappeared, totally causing some 2,000 dead. However, the typhoon brought one good thing. It washed a lot of the residual radiation into the sea and radiation levels fell thereafter.

Considering the enormous scale of destruction, the early attempts to re-establish a semblance of normal civic life on the scorched earth of the hypocenter seemed to be impossible. There also came a rumor saying that nothing would grow in Hiroshima for 75 years. Questions, such as whether reconstruction work of Hiroshima was possible in the first place, were frequently put forward. However, there was a desperate need for a more comprehensive plan to recover the city after the bombing. On 2 September, a few weeks after the end of the war, the earliest proposal of reconstructing Hiroshima into a peaceful city was put forward by Takano, the one who once announced to restore Hiroshima as soon as possible to continue functioning as a military base for the nation during the wartime.

In January 1946, the year when Takano resigned, a reconstruction department and the Reconstruction Council of Hiroshima City were established by the prefectural government. These two departments thereafter took an initiative to pave the way to reconstruct Hiroshima. Regarding the reconstruction plans and the future of Hiroshima, the new Governor of Hiroshima prefecture Tsunei Kusunose invited historian Yoshiro Saeki, novelist Yoko Ota, deputy Mayor of Kure city Tomiko Takara, and several others for a round-table discussion on 22 February 1946.

As governor, Mr. Kusunose put forward the ideas of short-term and long-term reconstruction work. He emphasized the urgency to carry out the short-term reconstruction, such as repairing streetcar lines, buildings, bridges and houses. While regarding the long-term work, the blueprint of future Hiroshima, Mr. Kusunose suggested collecting ideas from people all over the world. Instead of reconstructing Hiroshima into a great city, historian Saeki hoped to have Hiroshima follow a natural progression in its development, and novelist Ota insisted providing proper living facilities for A-bomb survivors should be put at the first place.

In contrast, Kure Mayor Takara suggested establishing a memorial graveyard at the burnt-out area for world peace, while reconstructing the new Hiroshima city in a different location. Anticipating such negative perspectives, *Chugoku Shimbun* issued one editorial claiming that "All of us, the homeland lovers, are unsatisfied with the irresponsible idea that the devastated city of Hiroshima should serve as a war memorial and be preserved eternally as a complete ruin. On the contrary, to establish a powerful great Hiroshima in the future, we shall start our reconstruction work right on the land and guard the land of our ancestors with strong determination".

Driven by the strong will to transform Hiroshima into a peaceful city, 34 proposals of city reconstruction plans were put forward by citizens, government officials, and people overseas. After a long-term careful discussion and processing, eventually in the fall of 1946, the official plan for city reconstruction was determined. In November 1945, the National Government established the War Damage Reconstruction Institute to promote reconstruction of cities damaged in World War II, and in September the following year the Special Town Planning Law was enacted. As one of the 115 war-damaged cities, Hiroshima was eligible to receive aid under the Special Law. Thereafter, its reconstruction work started with its most attainable goal of developing urban infrastructure—roads and parks.

The first step was road planning. The roads were partly based on the pre-war road system, while adding on new transport routes. In the end, a grid system was made that connected commercial and residential districts to the industrial one. Notable routes include the 100-meter-wide boulevard which ran through the center of the city from east to west and was later renamed the Peace Boulevard. The other decision was the planning of parks and green areas. In the plan that was proposed and acknowledged by the City Planning Commission, Hiroshima consisted of 3 large parks, 4 green areas, and 40 small parks. Riverbank green belts were also planned to "beautify the waterfront city".

However, the lack of financial aid delayed the implementation of the entire reconstruction project. At the time, the Japanese Government itself was on the verge of bankruptcy, with many other cities in desperate need of reconstruction funds. Due to the loss of all the revenue sources during the war and the inflation that followed the end of the war, Hiroshima found itself in dire financial straits. Citizens and those who were involved in the reconstruction work had to bear extreme hardship. Except for economic hardship, the lack of human resources as well as the shortage in both materials and public land also stood as obstacles to undertake the reconstruction of Hiroshima city.

Establishment of Legislation for Peace

Thanks to the efforts paid by civilian groups and local governmental officials, the turning point came in 1949, when Hiroshima's special status was made to be recognized by the National Government, and the Hiroshima Peace Memorial City Construction Law was passed. In accordance with this Law, the official plan of reconstructing Hiroshima into a city of peace was adopted in March 1952. Thereafter, the Peace Memorial Park, as well as other memorial facilities, including the Peace Memorial Museum and the Cenotaph for the A-bomb Victims, were to be constructed to manifest the city's genuine desire for lasting peace.

In early 1948, several citizen groups were formed in Hiroshima, aiming to convince the Japanese National Government to release former military land for civilian purposes. Embracing the same hope to continue the reconstruction work, Shinzo Hamai, the first popularly elected post-war Mayor of Hiroshima, was determined to convince the National Government to enact a special legislation regarding the status of Hiroshima. Because for Mayor Hamai, rebuilding Hiroshima as an international city of peace was a task that needed to be carried out in the name of the nation. To achieve the goal, he made numerous trips to the Japanese National Diet in Tokyo along with his secretary Chimata Fujimoto and chair of the Hiroshima City Council Tsukasa Nitoguri. Following the parliamentary election of January 1949, the initiative gained support from the ruling Liberal Party under Shigeru Yoshida.

In February 1949, Nitoguri visited Tadashi Teramitsu, then Director General of the Proceedings Department of the Upper House, and consulted him on actions they should take to move the reconstruction plan of Hiroshima forward. Teramitsu, a Hiroshima native who was familiar with Diet proceedings and knowledgeable about the legislative procedures, knew that a special law for local autonomies could be drafted. Aware of the challenges that were faced to pass the law such as the approval of the GHQ, Teramitsu was struggling with the right wording to get America's approval and crafted the law very carefully. The essence of the law was said by Teramitsu: "The Law will not only enable Hiroshima to recover from the war damage, but it will promote the idea of 'lasting peace', on which all human beings have fixed their minds. The central government will cooperate fully in the 'creation' of a city of peace, and the citizens of Hiroshima will also exert themselves to that end."

To some extent, it can be understood that Teramitsu's intention of reconstructing Hiroshima as "a peace memorial city" was due to Hiroshima's desperate need of financial aid from the National Government to continue its reconstruction plan. In the meantime, Mayor Hamai put enormous efforts into winning the approval from the GHQ as he wrote in one letter saying: "On 6 August 1945, the city of Hiroshima was reborn." This narrative of Hiroshima as a born-again city of peace was encouraged by local American commanders, who supported the idea of "reconstructing Hiroshima as a symbol of international peace". Although Hiroshima sacrificed itself for bringing peace, it was the Americans who made it happen and should be credited for ending the war to embrace peace.

This interpretation fully matched with the proposal that John D. Montgomery, then Kure-based Lieutenant, produced. Early in May 1946, Mayor Hamai sent a request to the occupation forces commanded by General Douglas MacArthur asking for an advisor to the Hiroshima City Reconstruction Planning Commission. Lieutenant Montgomery volunteered and became the emissary to convey Hiroshima's reconstruction requests to the American and Japanese authorities in Tokyo. Despite the lack of American and Japanese cooperation, Montgomery in June 1946 initiated a proposal of making Hiroshima a symbol of international peace and constructing a museum and a memorial tower at the hypocenter. However, they were not for commemorating peace, but for celebrating the baptism of America's first dropping of the atomic bomb and the ending of World War II which resulted in the birth of eternal peace.

With the intent to respond to the world's hope for reconstructing Hiroshima as a city for world peace, together with the hope that it would ease the anti-U.S. sentiment among the citizens of Hiroshima, the GHQ's head of political division, Justin Williams, approved the new law. Eventually in May 1949, after lengthy negotiations with the central government and the GHQ, the National Diet agreed to a law which was to express the commonly shared plan to rebuild Hiroshima city as "a peace memorial city". The law to that effect was passed in the Lower House on 10 May 1949, and in the Upper House the following day. For the law to become effective, it also required approval by municipal referendum, which was ended with approval of the new law.

On 6 August 1949, the fourth anniversary of the Hiroshima atomic bombing, the Hiroshima Peace Memorial City Construction Law was officially promulgated and enforced as a special law under Article 95 of the Constitution of Japan [Fig.4-1, Fig.4-2]. As stated in Article 1, the primary goal of the law was to construct Hiroshima into "a peace memorial city", rather than rebuilding it as the other war-torn cities did throughout Japan. This special identity as a city of peace granted by the law dramatically shifted the perception of Hiroshima from a painful reminder of destruction to a hopeful monument of everlasting peace. The result also reflected a shared interest between the U.S. occupation forces and the Japanese Government. While the former wanted to dissociate Hiroshima's disaster from the U.S.'s use of the atomic bomb, and the latter hoped to deny any causal relationship between the atomic bombing and Japan's aggression in Asia. Precisely speaking, the narrative of Hiroshima peace was not merely about "reborn", but more likely a deliberate amnesia about the wartime suffering of both Hiroshima and its Asian neighbors.

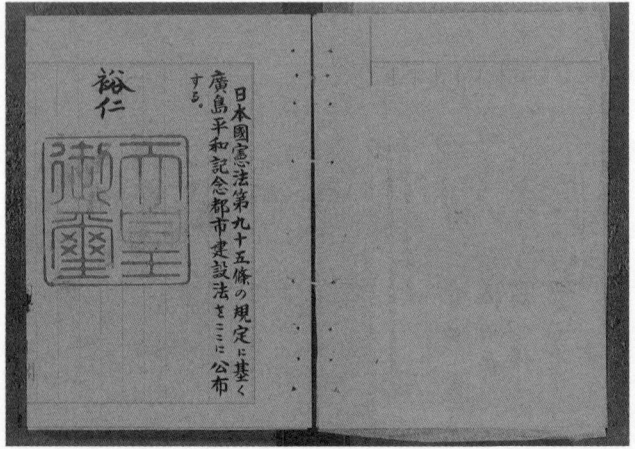

Fig.4-1 The front page of the Hiroshima Peace Memorial City Construction Law

Fig.4-2 Hiroshima Peace Memorial City 8-yen stamp in memory of the promulgation and enactment of the Hiroshima Peace Memorial City Construction Law, 6 August 1949

Apart from the symbolic aspects, the enactment of the Law contributed enormously to the full-scale reconstruction and development of Hiroshima city. Notifying the reconstruction of Hiroshima as a national project, the Law urged the National Government to provide more financial aid and subsidies. Except for the National Government, the local prefectural and municipal governments and other relevant departments were also required to provide every assistance for the reconstruction work. However, the main responsibility and the actual realization remained on a local level, since all measures for implementing works were assigned to the mayor's incumbency. In other words, the law stressed a close cooperation between officials and citizens, but at the same time it left all final decisions in the hands of the city administration, especially the mayor.

Most importantly, the Law paved the way to establish the Peace Memorial City Construction Plan, which replaced the previous plans made in 1946. Officially adopted in March 1952, the Plan approved two proposals on facility construction. One focused on constructing transportation, sanitation, safety, economic and other urban public facilities. For instance, the Plan formulated the large portion of public spaces furbished in greens, trying to cater the psychological needs of citizens in the post-war development. While the other involved the construction of peace memorial and other cultural facilities as would fit a peace memorial city, such as the construction of the Peace Memorial Park, the Cenotaph for the A-bomb Victims, and the Peace Memorial Museum, etc.

Construction of Space for Peace

Hiroshima Peace Memorial Park

Following the establishment of the 1949 Hiroshima Peace Memorial City Construction Law, a special project for constructing "peace memorial facilities" was approved. On 6 August 1949, when the Law was enacted, the City of Hiroshima made its decision to have the whole Nakajima District be home to "peace memorial facilities". Nakajima District had once been the city's busiest downtown commercial and residential district but was devastated in a single moment with all the lives vanished together, since it was the closest area to the hypocenter [Fig.4-3]. Hiroshima Peace Memorial Park was the first official attempt to memorialize the unprecedented use of the atomic bomb and to commemorate the end of the destructive war. Thus, its construction became one of the most significant projects.

Fig.4-3 Small-scale recreation of Nakajima District in Hiroshima before and after the atomic bombing on 6 August 1945

Before the location was finalized, an architecture competition for the Peace Memorial Park was announced by the architectural journal *Kenchiku Zasshi* early in May. The objective of this competition was "to respond to the worldwide movement for the establishment of a symbolic peace city". The competition briefly indicated that the park complex should comprise various facilities including a peace hall, a conference hall, an exhibition space, a bell tower, and offices, among other structures. A specific style was not designated, except for the stipulation that the design should suit the environment of the surrounding area. Out of the total 132 entries, Kenzo Tange's plan of featuring a large-scale park complex near the hypocenter won the first prize in the competition.

Prior to the competition, in the fall of 1946, at the request of the War Damage Rehabilitation Board, Tange went to Hiroshima volunteering on the contaminated site of the nuclear blast. He conducted a survey to assess the damage of the city and proposed a land-use plan that was partially integrated in the Hiroshima Reconstruction Plan of 1947. Despite the danger posed by residual radiation on the site, Tange was motivated to reconstruct the city, by his memories of attending secondary school there, and by the coincidence that his mother had been killed by an incendiary bomb at Imabari, his birthplace, on the day that Hiroshima was bombed.

His proposal was characterized by an axial composition and harmonized with the comprehensive urban structure of the city. The idea of "axis", east-west and north-south, came from the geographical features of the Hiroshima Delta. Defined by the Chugoku Mountains, the delta extends from east to west, together with the Otagawa River running from north toward south. Following this natural structure, the existing 100-meter-wide boulevard was used as an access road to establish the east-west axis, while the A-bomb Dome on the axis in line with the Cenotaph for the A-bomb Victims and the Peace Memorial Museum was settled as the north-south axis.

Having the east-west axis vertically integrated with the north-south axis, this design eventually became the prototype of the Peace Memorial Park. Viewed as a compass, the vertical integration points towards the four cardinal directions symbolizing the wholeness. It implies that Hiroshima tries to send peace messages through every possible direction to the whole world. Given that Tange himself was a Catholic, some see this vertical integration as the Cross in Christianity, while others consider it has a structure similar to Itsukushima Shrine. Embracing such religious symbolization, this vertical integration is also interpreted as a religious monument to commemorate the souls perished and to protect the city from future destruction.

However, the government-led reconstruction work did not progress smoothly, as it left the civilians' suffering completely behind the scenes. When the construction was about to begin, there were around 400 illegal shacks on the site. The prefectural and municipal offices shared their responsibilities for clearing 120 and 280 shacks respectively. But when the ground was leveled for construction, many human bones were exposed. Furthermore, there were many survivors living in the shacks, as Keiji Nakazawa recalled in his book "*Hiroshima*" *no Kuhaku* (The Blank of Hiroshima): "…the shacks were what we could find and build to sustain our lives. When we heard even the shacks would be destroyed, we trembled with anger. Using the beautiful word 'Peace', the old-fashioned authorities once again hurt the A-bomb survivors. What a Peace City! How ridiculous!"

Fig.4-4 Hiroshima Peace Memorial Park, 20 September 2008

In this way, people's welfare was involuntarily sacrificed to serve the construction of the Peace Memorial Park, which was completed in the late 1950s [Fig.4-4]. Overall, the park covers approximately 122,100 square meters, with the 100-meter-wide Peace Boulevard traversing the city center and running along the park's southern boundary [Fig.4-5]. In the park, there are a great number of memorials, monuments, public facilities, and several A-bombed trees, dedicated to commemorating the atomic bomb victims and every survivor who has since passed away, as well as to conveying the horrors of nuclear weapons and advocating world peace.

Fig.4-5 Peace Boulevard tablet

Hiroshima Peace Memorial Museum

In Tange's prizewinning design for the Hiroshima Peace Memorial Park, the construction of a peace memorial museum was also proposed. The Museum was crucial to the plan, as it served as the central feature where form and content were fused. To intersect the 100-meter-wide Peace Boulevard and the A-bomb Dome, Tange designed the museum with its axis running through the park. As it acted as a gateway to the park, the pilotis were carefully placed to allow for the view down the major axis. In 1951, work on the Hiroshima Peace Memorial Museum (today's Main Building) started. As work began, Tange had refined the design from its initial vision, improving it and placing the museum at the center of the complex.

The Museum (Main Building) turned out to be a long, narrow, geometrical, single-story building, constructed of reinforced concrete structural frame and glass windows [Fig.4-6]. It is raised above the ground on 6.5-meter-tall rectangular pilotis and entered by a staircase piercing the lower horizontal cantilevered slab floor. Both the exterior and interior of the

Fig.4-6 Hiroshima Peace Memorial Museum (Main Building)

museum are finished in rough concrete, so as not to distract the visitors from the content of the exhibition. The typically modernist austerity and modularity also recalls traditional Japanese architecture.

In general, the mission of the Peace Memorial Museum is to serve as a space where individuals can gain an accurate and vivid picture of the A-bomb attack by recording the tragic and terrible effects of the bombing and subsequent radiation. Among more than 21,000 historical items and documents collected from the officials, survivors, and remaining families, some 200 items are displayed as a permanent exhibit. These items range from personal belongings and daily necessities to the remainder of A-bombed buildings. Since its opening, it has been the most popular of Hiroshima's destinations for school field trips from all over Japan and for international visitors. According to the Hiroshima Peace Culture Foundation, over 74.76 million people visited the museum from its opening in 1955 through 2021, averaging over 1.1 million visitors per year.

By mid-2019, the museum had undergone three renovations. The first renovation, in 1975, was conducted to repair the aging structure and keep the materials from deteriorating, as well as to redesign the exhibition contents. In 1994, the second renovation was carried out aiming to provide more space for peace education. As a result, the museum was expanded into two buildings: Main Building and East Building [Fig.4-7]. The Main Building conveys what happened on 6 August 1945 through scientific explanations and exhibits of items belonging to the victims. The East Building tells the story of Hiroshima before and after the bombing and the city's nuclear disarmament efforts.

Fig.4-7 Main Building (middle) and East Building (right) of the Hiroshima Peace Memorial Museum in line with Hiroshima International Conference Center (left)

Fig.4-8 Exhibition of remains left by children who were killed in the bombing

The third renovation was a huge project for both buildings. Beginning with the East Building and then the Main Building, the renovation work lasted from 2014 to 25 April 2019. Reopened on 26 April 2017, the East Building features more interactive displays and replaces the model of the city with a new version that uses projection mapping to demonstrate the effects of the bomb blast. Reopened on 25 April 2019, the Main Building renovates the permanent exhibits to focus more on victims' belongings [Fig.4-8, Fig.4-9].

Fig.4-9 Exhibition of rubble and bicycle after the bombing

Fig.4-10 Being left untreated, most of the victims were on the brink of death. Drawing by Shoichi Furukawa (aged 32 at the time of bombing, 62 when he drew the picture)

Overall, after the third renovation, the permanent exhibits present in both buildings are divided into six sections. In sequential order, they are (1) "Introduction Exhibit"; (2) "Hiroshima on 6 August", (3) "Victims and Survivors" and (4) "Gallery"; (5) "Dangers of Nuclear Weapons" and (6) "Hiroshima History". In the East Building, there are also video testimonies of the A-bomb survivors and temporary exhibitions held in the special exhibition room on the first floor and in the temporary exhibition room in the basement. Additionally, the museum has also created an online peace database, where A-bomb related photos, drawings by A-bomb survivors and other artistic works can be found [Fig.4-10].

In terms of the current exhibition, there are three thought-provoking points worth mentioning. First, the section where panels on "Hiroshima and War" are located has been readjusted. Before the 2019 renovation, the panels were included in the first section "Introduction Exhibit", but now they have been moved to the closing section "Hiroshima History". Since the 1994 renovations when the museum acknowledged Japanese aggression in Asia, panels depicting Hiroshima as an important military base together with its civilians' wartime effort had been included in the first section. The Nanjing Massacre was also included, with a picture showing how Hiroshima citizens celebrated the fall of Nanjing. However, today all the panels referring to Hiroshima's wartime status have been relocated to the closing section. As the previous five sections cover a vast amount of information, it is of high possibility that visitors will ignore it simply due to the running out of time and patience. On my visit to the museum in January 2020, there were few visitors who spent time at the closing section.

Second, regarding the exhibitions on A-bomb survivors, new narratives introducing non-Japanese A-bomb survivors have been added through wall panels and big photos of three non-Japanese: an elderly Korean, a student from Malaysia and a German priest. It is an improvement comparing with the museum's previous narratives, but as Jeff Kingston, a professor of History and Director of Asian Studies based in Japan, wrote in his reviewing article on the museum's latest renovation, "since Korean forced laborers were the largest foreign-born ethnic group working in Hiroshima, there is still an inadequate recognition of the far larger-scale deaths of Koreans". Furthermore, these disparate groups are gathered in the same corner only because they were all non-Japanese, while the varied experience and stories remain largely untold and unappreciated. In other words, the museum fails to dignify their humanity in the way it does so for the Japanese casualties.

In addition, regarding the Japanese A-bomb survivors there is a section named "The Breakdown of Family N", of which the photos are all taken by Kikujiro Fukushima, one of the hardest critics on Hiroshima. The museum presents these photos, together with the story of Sadako Sasaki as a set, only seeking to strengthen the extreme sufferings that the atomic bombing brought to the people. However, the panels make no reference to the unfairness the victims experienced after being diagnosed with A-bomb diseases and their death because of being abandoned by the Government in terms of medical and welfare services, like the involuntary sacrifice survivors had to bear for the sake of the construction of the park. Such misleading re-interpretation created by the museum is quite different from the original intention of Kikujiro Fukushima, as he stated in his book *Pikadon* that the Hiroshima Peace Memorial Museum didn't want to display his work because he had always been critical about the city.

Third, some panels in the fifth section "Dangers of Nuclear Weapons", especially those depicting the end of the war, somehow reflect a revisionist view of history. According to Prof. Kingston, the museum doesn't reflect on the responsibility of Japan's military or imperial elites, rather it assigns all responsibility to the U.S., for both the failure to end the war before the atomic bombings and the Soviet Union entry into the war. Furthermore, omissions and distortions regarding the development of the war somehow presents a biased narrative. For example, there is a panel mentioning that the Japanese triggered the war with its surprise attack on Pearl Harbor, but the far more massive Japanese War of Aggression against China that had escalated since 1931 is not mentioned nor is the Japanese aggression in the other parts of Asia.

Notable Peace Symbols inside the Park

A-bomb Dome

In a similar manner, omissions considering the history of the primary landmark of the Peace Memorial Park, A-bomb Dome, also happen. Originally serving as the Hiroshima Prefectural Industrial Promotion Hall, A-bomb Dome was the structure left standing closest to the hypocenter. It was preserved as a witness to the horror of nuclear weapons, a memorial to the people who were killed in the atomic bombing and the most significant as an appeal for world peace. Designated as a UNESCO World Heritage Site, its identity as a symbol of Hiroshima's pledge to seek lasting peace was further confirmed. However, its history of contributing to the Japanese imperialism's economic expansion is beautifully erased.

During the Sino-Japanese War of 1894-1895, the Imperial Headquarters was set up at the site of today's A-bomb Dome, dispatching soldiers to Korea and China. This huge amount of military demand linked with the Sino-Japanese War of 1894-1895 and Russo-Japanese War greatly helped Hiroshima's economy thrive. In April 1915, the hall was constructed as a facility for the display and sale of commercial products within Hiroshima prefecture. Designed by a Czech architect Jan Letzel (1880-1926), the hall was established using a brick construction partially reinforced with a steel frame, having the exterior wall be made of stones and mortar. Being a grand European style, the main body was a three-story building with a five-story stairwell capped with an oval shaped copper dome in the center of the entrance hall [Fig.4-11]. Formally open to the public in August, the hall was first named the

Fig.4-11 **Hiroshima Prefectural Industrial Promotion Hall in its original condition during the Taisho Period**

Hiroshima Prefectural Commercial Exhibition Hall. In January 1921, its name was changed to the Hiroshima Prefectural Product Exhibition Hall, and finally in November 1933, to the Hiroshima Prefectural Industrial Promotion Hall.

Located in the large business district, this modern hall was extensively used for about 30 years till it was ruined in 1945. It started with introducing products from Hiroshima prefecture and nearby prefectures, aiming to promote local commerce and culture. At the same time, it also functioned as a museum and art gallery. During wartime, special exhibitions, such as the Japan-Manchuria Trade Exhibition, were held in the hall. As the war intensified around 1944, the building served as the offices of the Interior Ministry's Chugoku-Shikoku Public Works, the Hiroshima District Lumber Control Corporation, and other national and municipal organizations, and regulated associations.

On 6 August 1945, the atomic bomb exploded 150 meters horizontally from the hall, thus it was heavily damaged and completely burned [Fig.4-12]. Around 30 people in the building were killed instantly. But as the explosion was almost directly overhead, the building was able to retain its dome's iron frame and thus its symbolic appearance and its name today. In 1953, management of the site was transferred from Hiroshima prefecture to Hiroshima city. By then, how to incorporate Hiroshima's tragic history within its post-war reincarnation turned out to be a dilemma among city planners. Some officials favored removing every physical remnant of the tragedy, while others insisted on preserving the evidence of the atomic bomb's destructive power. The A-bomb Dome became a hot subject of debate.

Fig.4-12 A-bomb Dome among the ruins of buildings in Hiroshima in early October 1945

From 1950 through 1964, the Hiroshima Peace Memorial Park was established around the A-bomb Dome. Ultimately on 11 July 1966, a resolution on the permanent preservation of the A-bomb Dome was adopted by the Hiroshima City Council, claiming "it was one of our duties to preserve the Dome not only for commemorating those perished in the bombing but also for the hope of world peace". As a result, the ruin was officially named Hiroshima Peace Memorial and fund-raising for the preservation work was carried out domestically and internationally. Through the efforts of the civic society, preservation work on the A-bomb Dome was completed in 1967. The ruin had been preserved in the same state as immediately after the bombing [Fig.4-13]. In the following years, two minor preservation projects were carried out to stabilize the ruin, respectively in October 1989 and March 1990.

Fig.4-13 **A-bomb Dome across the Motoyasu River**

Further calls from the city and the local citizens to have the site listed as a World Heritage arose in June 1992, when Japan signed the World Heritage Convention. Gaining support from the Hiroshima City Council, the movement turned into a full-scale campaign. In January 1993, Hiroshima's mayor formally requested the National Government to recommend the A-bomb Dome to be registered on the World Heritage List. In June, the Committee to Promote the A-bomb Dome as a World Heritage was established, receiving a great deal of support from citizens' groups. The committee later launched a nationwide signature drive and gathered over 1.65 million people signing for the A-bomb Dome to be registered as a World Heritage. Eventually, the efforts from both civil society and local government paid off in 1996. With its history starting from 6 August 1945, the A-bomb Dome entered the 21st century being a legacy of peace common to the entire humankind.

Cenotaph for the A-bomb Victims

Aligned to the A-bomb Dome, almost the center of the Peace Memorial Park, there stands the Cenotaph for the A-bomb Victims (hereinafter referred to as the A-bomb Cenotaph) [Fig.4-14]. Its official name is Memorial Monument for Hiroshima, City of Peace. Designed in 1952 by Kenzo Tange, it is an arch-shaped monument holding the names of all those killed by the atomic bombing. Being one of the first memorial monuments built on an open field, it was unveiled during the Peace Memorial Ceremony on 6 August 1952. Made of reinforced concrete, the Cenotaph deteriorated badly after 32 years of its construction. In June 1984, the remodeling construction of a new cenotaph began and was eventually completed on 26 March 1985. The new Cenotaph was reconstructed by Inada Stone and kept the same size and shape as the original one.

Fig.4-14 A-bomb Cenotaph

Walking closer to the A-bomb Cenotaph, you can see the A-bomb Dome through the Cenotaph. It is a perfectly symmetric frame to capture the dome which symbolizes the massive destruction that the bomb caused to Hiroshima and its people. Being designed in the shape of an ancient Japanese clay house, the A-bomb Cenotaph represents a shelter for the souls of those who perished in the atomic bombing out of rain. This intention derives from the fact that many people were exposed to the high-level of radiation from the Black Rain that did continue for several days after the bombing. Meanwhile, the Cenotaph also looks like half of an eye staring at the A-bomb Dome, which could be interpreted as the deceased souls are always watching their descendants from the sky, while they keep the other half of their eyes on what Hiroshima and the rest of the world are doing for promoting peace.

Under the Cenotaph at the center there is a stone chamber, housing the register of the names of deceased A-bomb victims, regardless of nationality. Through the application procedures, relatives of the deceased can have the victims' names be added to the register. According to the City of Hiroshima, as of 6 August 2022, the register comprises 123 volumes holding 333,907 names of those who perished both in Hiroshima and Nagasaki. Of the 123 volumes, 121 contain the names of those deceased in Hiroshima. One volume holds the names of 13 victims of the Nagasaki atomic bombing whose family requested to have their names be included in the register dedicated to the memorial cenotaph in Hiroshima. The rest one volume bears the names of those unknown with the words "many people whose names are unknown" on it.

In front of the stone chamber, there is a monument. On it carves the inscription in Japanese: "安らかに眠って下さい 過ちは繰り返しませぬから" (Let all the souls here rest in peace; For we shall not repeat the evil), by Tadayoshi Saika, professor of English Literature at Hiroshima University. As an A-bomb survivor himself, Prof. Saika's fear and hatred over the atomic bombing were no less than the rest of the survivors. As a teacher, he also deeply regretted encouraging his students to the battlefield during the war. In the initial writing, he intended to express the idea that all human beings, including the Japanese, must vow never to repeat the evil of war. It is "we" human beings who made the tragedy happen and it is "we" who must make the pledge to lasting peace. Bearing the dual moral responsibilities, he sought to send peace messages to the entire world from a perspective that encompasses the past, the present and the future.

When the inscription was settled, controversies over it arose. To clarify the message that the inscription contained, Prof. Saika contributed a letter to city officials saying: "...the citizens of Hiroshima are not brooding on the past. Instead, we are longing for a bright future and attempting to search for genuine peace... If the efforts made by Hiroshima brighten the future, then the sacrifice made by the victims has not been in vain." In other words, the word "we" refers to the entire human race, while "evil" means the misuse of the atomic bombs. A-bomb victims, regardless of nationalities, should be recognized as a foundation of peace for all human beings. No more nuclear weapons should not merely be the earnest hope of the victims but also of all humanity on earth. However, such interpretation once again seems to reflect that an amnesia of Japan's past aggression is there to cover up its troubled history, which is not easy to be accepted by people in Asia.

Cenotaph for Korean A-bomb Victims

One group of Asian people who may be resistant to the controversial inscription of the A-bomb Cenotaph are Koreans, especially Zainichi Koreans (ethnic Korean residents in Japan). Since the Meiji Period, Japan had started its colonization of the Korean Empire indirectly and directly. During wartime, a vast number of Koreans were involuntarily sent to Japan, either through forced service or conscription, to make up the labor shortage. Toward the end of the war, approximately 3 million Koreans were living in Japan. Among them, around 100,000 were dispatched to Hiroshima city. Some were in service to the Imperial Japanese Army as soldiers and civilian workers, while others were slave laborers conscripted by the Japanese Government for industrial work.

During their stay in Japan, Koreans were discriminated against in one way or another. Even when they died, their corpses were discriminated against too. As Michiko Ishimure, a Japanese writer and peace activist, wrote: "After the bomb, the last corpses to be disposed of were the Koreans. Many Japanese survived the bomb, but very few Koreans did...The crows came and ate the eyeballs of the Korean corpses. They ate the eyeballs." According to the inscription on the Cenotaph for Korean A-bomb Victims, around 20,000 Koreans perished in the Hiroshima atomic bombing. On the other hand, some estimated that about 10 percent of the total number of those who died in the atomic bombing had Korean lineage, which would amount to about 30,000.

Fig.4-15 Cenotaph for Korean A-bomb Victims in the Peace Memorial Park

Decorated with Korean national symbols, the Cenotaph for Korean A-bomb Victims was established to commemorate Korean victims and survivors of the atomic bombing on 10 April 1970. Initiated by the Korean Residents Union (also known as Mindan) in Japan, the monument standing on a turtle-shaped base engraved with the epigraph "Souls of the dead ride to heaven on the backs of turtles" is 5 meters high. On the monument there reads the inscription: "the Monument in Memory of the Korean Victims of the A-bomb: the souls of His Highness Prince Yi Wu (a member of the Korean Royal family who served for the Japanese Imperial Army during wartime) and over 20,000 others." At the top of the obelisk there is a crown sculpted with two dragons, in which the names of Korean victims of the A-bomb were stored [Fig.4-15].

Unfortunately, the discrimination continued. Originally, the monument was erected near the Aioi Bridge, the site where the body of Prince Yi Wu was found, because the Hiroshima municipal government refused to allow the monument to be placed inside the Peace Memorial Park. Since then, criticism over the placement of the monument intensified. The most significant assertion had been that it was a manifestation of ethnic discrimination toward Koreans and Zainichi Koreans. Regarding the matter, the municipal government once had offered to build a separate monument for all Korean victims but was held up by the disagreement over the inscription and design of the monument among the concerned parties. Eventually on 24 December 1998, as the 1994 Peace Memorial Museum renovation acknowledged Japanese aggression in Asia, an agreement was reached to move the monument into the Peace Memorial Park. Thanks to the persistent effort made by the civilian groups involved, today the monument stands inside the Peace Memorial Park.

Children's Peace Monument

Speaking of people power, the construction of the Children's Peace Monument (Genbaku no Ko no Zo) was also made possible by civilian groups, especially the children. Initially, the proposal of building the monument was put forward by a group of students, who were shocked by the death of Sadako Sasaki. At the age of two, Sadako Sasaki was exposed to the atomic bombing at home, which was about 1.7 kilometers away from the hypocenter. Immediately blown out of the window, she was found alive by her mother without any apparent injuries. While escaping from the big fire with her mother, they were caught in black rain. Years later, she was diagnosed with leukemia (later it was referred to as atomic bomb disease) and was told to have no longer than one year to live. Strongly advised by the doctor, she began her hospitalization in the Hiroshima Red Cross Hospital.

Fig.4-16 Origami cranes

As a result, she had to quit school life, where she was popular among her classmates and was active in sports meetings as relay player. This sudden change was not only a great shock to her family but also to her classmates. Taking turns, they went to visit Sadako in the hospital every day. During Sadako's hospitalization, she spent most of her time folding origami cranes driven by the ancient Japanese legend promising that anyone who folds a thousand origami cranes within one year will be granted a wish [Fig.4-16]. Unfortunately, her simple wish to live through the disease was not achieved and she eventually died of leukemia on 25 October 1955.

Sad news of the death of Sadako drove her friends and schoolmates to cry out for peace. They decided to build a monument to remember Sadako as well as the other child victims of the atomic bombs. Quickly, a children's fundraising campaign was initiated and led by the students, which made the idea spread all over the nation and collected donations from over 3,200 schools and even gained support from overseas. Directly at the base of the monument, there is a black granite slab on which it carved the words written by a junior high school student in Japanese: "これはぼくらの叫びです。これはわたしたちの祈りです。世界に平和をきずくための" (This is our cry. This is our prayer. For building peace in this world) [Fig.4-17].

Fig.4-17 Inscription on the slab at the base of the Children's Peace Monument

Fig.4-18 Children's Peace Monument

Designed by the native artists Kazuo Kikuchi and Kiyoshi Ikebe, the 9-meter-high monument was unveiled on 5 May 1958, the Japanese Children's Day. A bronze statue of a young girl modeled after Sadako stands at the very top, stretching her arms up in the sky holding a golden origami crane, longing for world peace [Fig.4-18]. The design well tells Sadako's story of folding origami cranes, which became widely known and was made into a film called *Senbazuru* (Thousand Origami Cranes) in 1989. Sadako's story also attracts schools and many other individuals all around the world sending origami cranes to the monument in memory of Sadako and other child victims. Today, origami crane has become a symbol of peace. Each year, approximately 10 million origami cranes are dedicated to the Children's Peace Monument.

On the left and right flank, there are two other figures, symbolizing a boy and a girl together hoping for a bright and peaceful future. Hanging inside the monument there is a traditional peace bell, and beneath it suspends a bronze crane. When pushing the crane against the bell, the sound of a wind chime will be produced [Fig.4-19]. These two pieces were donated by Dr. Hideki Yukawa, winner of the Nobel Prize for Physics, who was deeply touched by the children's movement.

Fig.4-19 The bronze crane and the peace bell of the monument

Development of Ritual for Peace

The overall construction of spaces for peace greatly contributes to the Hiroshima Peace Memorial Ceremony being held every year on 6 August, the A-bomb Day, in front of the A-bomb Cenotaph. Organized by the City of Hiroshima, some 50,000 local citizens and visitors, including the families of the deceased, ambassadors, and dignitaries from around 70 countries, gather to console the souls of those perished in the atomic bombing as well as every survivor who has since passed away and to pray for the abolition of nuclear weapons and the realization of everlasting world peace.

Held virtually every year since 1947, the ceremony features speeches with entreaties for peace from the Prime Minister of Japan, the Mayor of Hiroshima, and other noteworthy figures. (Except for the year of 1950 when the Korean War broke out and it was not allowed to take place by the U.S. occupation.) At the exact time the atomic bomb was dropped, 8:15 in the morning of 6 August, the Peace Bell tolls. Siren sound reaches the whole city. Not merely people who are present at the ceremony, but also those who are in the households and workplaces will spend one minute silently praying for the deceased and for eternal world peace. The regular procedures of the Peace Memorial Ceremony last from 8:00 a.m. to 8:50 a.m.

As a matter of fact, the ceremony is part of the Peace Festival, which can date back to the first anniversary of the atomic bombing in 1946. The first plan "to mark out a sufficiently large territory close to the center of the atomic explosion and to keep it as a commemorative site" was announced by the prefectural government only a few weeks after the atomic bombing. But the survivors refused to wait for the official site of commemoration that eventually took another ten years to complete. Hence, for the first anniversary, citizens mourned for the dead at the local Gokoku Shrine and named it Peace Recovery Festival (Heiwa Fukko Sai).

The anniversary received wide international attention and thereby fostered awareness of the global relevance of the atomic bomb experience. Accordingly, the mayor felt the need to strengthen the international aspects through an overall Peace Festival (Heiwa Sai) to rebuild the city as the international city for world peace. Thus in 1947, the City of Hiroshima held the first three-day Hiroshima Peace Festival, with the hope to develop it into a global event to widely spread Hiroshima's sincere desire for a world without nuclear weapons domestically and internationally [Fig.4-20]. The festival started on 5 August and ended on 7 August. The main memorial ceremony was held, on 6 August, by the then Mayor Shinzo Hamai, in the area that eventually became the Peace Memorial Park.

Fig.4-20 A crowd of Japanese people during the Hiroshima Peace Festival, outside the A-bomb Cenotaph, 6 August 1952

During the first official Peace Memorial Ceremony, Mayor Hamai delivered a speech, which was established as an annual routine known as the Peace Declaration. Fulfilled with cries against war and prays for peace from the bottom of the hearts of the people of Hiroshima, Mayor Haimai delivered the first Peace Declaration, addressing: "This horrible weapon brought about a 'Revolution of Thought', which has convinced us of the necessity and the value of eternal peace…because of this atomic bomb, the people of the world have become aware that a global war in which atomic energy would be used would lead to the end of our civilization and extinction of mankind… Let us join in renouncing war eternally and building a plan for world peace on this earth." [Fig.4-21]

Since 1947, the Peace Declaration has been delivered by the Mayors of Hiroshima every year during the 6 August Peace Memorial Ceremony. At the same time, peace messages have been sent to every country around the world, spreading Hiroshima's wish for the abolition of nuclear weapons and the realization of eternal world peace. By the year of 2022, the Peace Declaration had encompassed a variety of peace related issues, such as a rejection of achieving peace by force, a total ban on atomic and hydrogen bombs, and the importance of passing on A-bomb experiences, etc. However, no mayor had ever mentioned the fact that it was the United States who dropped the atomic bomb on Hiroshima, and the highly controversial title of "the only A-bombed nation" had been frequently used in the Peace Declarations since the 1980s.

Every year, the content of the Peace Declaration changes over time. In 1956, a year after the First World Conference against Atomic and Hydrogen Bombs, the words "against atomic and hydrogen bombs" first appeared in Mayor Tadao Watanabe's Peace Declaration. In 1971, 26 years after the end of World War II, Mayor Setsuo Yamada emphasized in the Peace Declaration the great necessity of peace education to help to pass on the meaning of war and peace to the next generation. In 1982, Mayor Takeshi Araki appealed to the cities of the world in his Peace Declaration for the proposal of solidarity that was made at the Second UN Special Session for Disarmament in June of the same year.

Fig.4-21 Mayor Shinzo Hamai read the Peace Declaration during the first Peace Festival, 6 August 1947

Additionally, three Peace Declarations delivered by Mayor Takashi Hiraoka are worth mentioning. Mayor Hiraoka was the first ever Mayor of Hiroshima who expressed his regret for the people of Asia-Pacific region publicly. In 1991, the 50th anniversary of the start of the Pacific War, he addressed: "Japan inflicted great suffering and despair on the peoples of Asia and the Pacific during its reign of colonial domination in the war. There can be no excuse for these actions." In 1995, the 50th anniversary of the end of World War II, he stressed that the war must be reexamined from the perspectives of both perpetrator and victim. "It is important to look at the stark reality of war in terms of both the aggrieved and the aggressor to develop a common understanding of history. The suffering of all the war victims is indelibly etched in our hearts, and we want to apologize for the unbearable suffering that Japanese colonial domination and war inflicted on so many people." In the 1997 Peace Declaration, he further emphasized the necessity of candid dialogue amongst the people of the world to transcend differences in language, religion and custom.

Apart from the Peace Ceremony, on the evening of 6 August, a Peace Message Lantern Floating Ceremony (Toro Nagashi) is held around the park [Fig.4-22]. The site of today's Peace Memorial Park was a normally populated area where people worked and lived. When the atomic bomb was dropped, not everyone in close radius to the hypocenter was killed immediately. Many were severely burned by the heatwave but still managed to move. Most of them could not bear the pain and heat from the burns thus threw themselves into the river for relief. Unfortunately, most of them did not survive. Around 1948, some citizens started to float lanterns to console the souls of their friends and family members who had passed away in this river, which is a long traditional custom stemming from the Obon Festival in Japan.

Fig.4-22 Peace Message Lantern Floating Ceremony in Hiroshima, 6 August 2021

Throughout the whole process of reconstructing once a devastated city into today's city of peace, there had been a lot of inevitable difficulties and grieves, borne by the local government and its people, though in different aspects. Despite all the hardships, the transformation of Hiroshima is quite successful. Many lessons can be learned for those cities which are also striving to build themselves into a city of peace. However, the narrative of Hiroshima peace is largely based on its collective memory of traumatic events, especially the victimization caused by the atomic bombing. Addressing its history merely through a perspective of being a victim, while ignoring the perpetrator perspective, doubtlessly incurs controversies over its peace building process.

Chapter 5

Revisiting Hiroshima through a Peace Studies Lens

Peace Education and Peace Research

From the year Japan surrendered to 1952, its sovereignty was placed under the control of the GHQ, whose initial objectives were the demilitarization and democratization of Japan. What came to form the core of reforming was the establishment of the new Constitution in 1946, proclaiming both democracy and pacifism.

Clearly stated in the Preface, it says: "Government is a sacred trust of the people, and authority for which is derived from the people, the powers of which are exercised by the representative of the people, and the benefits of which are enjoyed by the people… We, the Japanese people, desire peace for all time and are deeply conscious of the high ideals controlling human relationships, and we have determined to preserve our security and existence, trusting in the justice and faith of the peace-loving peoples of the world. We desire to occupy an honored place in an international society striving for the preservation of peace…We recognize that all peoples of the world have the right to live in peace, free from fear and want."

In achieving the reconstruction of Japan and the rehabilitation of Japanese people, education reform became an integral part of the GHQ's strategy. Principally following the philosophy of the Constitution, the Fundamental Law of Education was launched in 1947, which concretely declares the role of education for the construction of a peaceful society. Represented in Article 1, it defines the aim of education: "Education shall aim at the full development of personality, striving to nurture the citizens, sound in mind and body, who shall love truth and justice, esteem individual value, respect labor and have a deep sense of responsibility, and be imbued with the independent spirit, as builders of the peaceful state and society."

To begin with, GHQ's Civil Information and Education (CIE) Section eliminated courses in history, geography, and morals that inculcated ultranationalist thought. Adopting the practice known as suminuri, any nationalistic, militaristic, authoritarian, or anti-American content was blackened out from the learning materials [Fig.5-1]. As the primary method of educational reform, suminuri (blackened-out) textbooks were used until the Ministry of Education (today the Ministry of Education, Culture, Sports, Science and Technology, abbreviated as MEXT) produced newly reformed ones. The focuses of the new texts were to condemn militarism and ultranationalism and encourage democratic habits of thought.

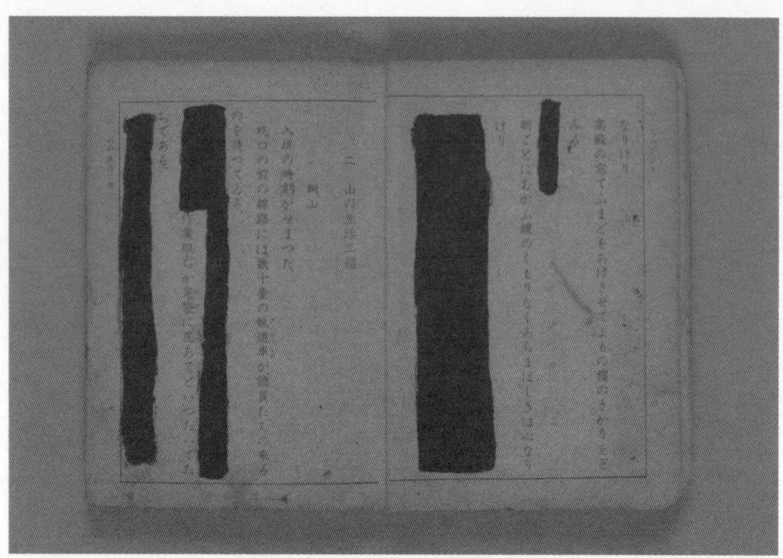

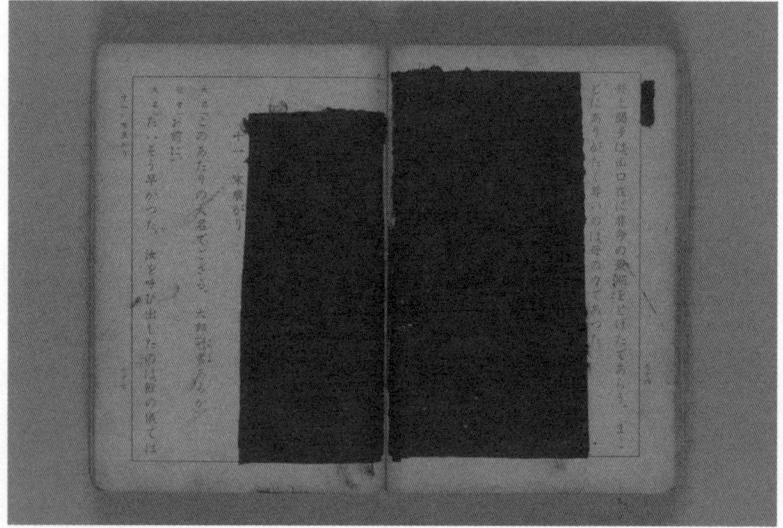

Fig.5-1 Suminuri textbook, August 1943

In promoting the newly reformed education, Japan Teachers Union (JTU) played a key role. Founded in 1947, it was the largest labor union of teachers and school staff, who often held its critical stance against the conservatives. At the outbreak of the Korean War in 1950, JTU created the slogan "Never Let Us Send Pupils and Students to the Battlefields Again!" It helped to make anti-war as the central focus of peace education for a while, but was soon suppressed by the U.S. occupation forces. Along with the history textbooks produced at the time, the basis of education to promote pacifism and democracy had always been condemning the militarist leadership for forcing the Japanese people into a reckless war and causing misery to the Japanese and other Asian peoples. In other words, the Japanese had only themselves to blame for the war and its consequences.

In opposition, conservatives argued that it had become so thorough in condemning ultranationalism and so radical in promoting liberals that younger generations were becoming deficient in patriotic sentiment and bereft of any moral foundation as Japanese. Therefore, since the independence of Japan in 1952, conservative groups have made repeated attempts to regain a measure of control over history and social studies textbook narratives. To provide a positive image of the nation for younger generations, textbooks were renewed tending to whitewash Japan's wartime aggression and dwell on Japan's own victimhood—the Hiroshima and Nagasaki atomic bombings.

As the censorship was lessened following the end of occupation, damages inflicted by the two atomic bombs in Hiroshima and Nagasaki started to be disclosed to the public. Along with the nationwide Anti-Nuclear Weapons Movement triggered by the 1954 Lucky Dragon Incident, media coverage of the nuclear devastation was further intensified. Eventually, the sufferings of Hiroshima and Nagasaki became the national victimhood of Japan. Many textbooks began to depict the Hiroshima and Nagasaki atomic bombings as unique experiences that invested the Japanese with an exclusive pacifist mission—the elimination of nuclear weapons worldwide.

Hiroshima Peace Education in General

Against such a background, the Hiroshima Municipal Board of Education distributed its first official guideline for peace education to elementary, junior high and senior high schools in 1968. Having suffered the terrible destruction wrought by the atomic bombing, the emphasis of Hiroshima's peace education naturally centered on its A-bomb victimization. Seeking to pass on the experiences of the A-bomb survivors to the younger generations in Japan and around the world, the Hiroshima Prefecture Hibakusha Teachers' Association was founded in 1969 to boost peace education.

Apart from the moral responsibility, Japan's active involvement in supporting the United States in the Korean War and the Vietnam War despite its Peace Constitution, as well as its establishment of Self-Defense Force and growing intention to expand warfare, further urged teachers to unite for promoting peace education. In 1971, with support from the JTU, Japan Hibakusha Teachers' Association (the National Liaison Committee of the Hibakusha Teachers' Associations) was established. In 1972, the Hiroshima Institute for Peace Education was set up to conduct research on teaching materials for developing a well-structured peace education curriculum.

According to the Hiroshima Municipal Board of Education, the framework of current peace education programs for Hiroshima municipal

elementary, junior high and senior high schools is as follows:
- Elementary School (Grade 1 to 3): To be aware of the actual state of the atomic bombing, the value of life and the love of humanity (picture books).
- Elementary School (Grade 4 to 6): To understand the actual state of the atomic bombing and the process of Hiroshima's recovery (A-bomb testimony).
- Junior High School: To study and examine issues or problems related to world peace.
- Senior High School: To cultivate prospects for the realization of world peace.

Since receptivity varies at different age levels, the content and material used to facilitate peace education are different. But the basis has largely been the experience of the atomic bombing, thus "world peace", as mentioned in the framework, can basically be understood as a peaceful world free of nuclear weapons.

In 1973, the first National Peace Education Symposium was held by JTU and Japan Hibakusha Teachers' Association in Hiroshima city, which led to the founding of Japan Council for Peace Education Research in the following year. Consequently, peace education was integrated into the national curriculum and started to be taught not only as a separate course but across several different subjects, such as social studies and Japanese literature. In 1976, a resolution to promote school trips to visit the A-bombed cities of Hiroshima and Nagasaki was adopted. Subsequently, the number of schools organizing school trips to Hiroshima and Nagasaki had rapidly increased. Hiroshima, the center of education during the pre-war period, now becomes the role model of Japan's peace education.

In 2004, regarding the aging of A-bomb survivors, their testimonies were collected and compiled as the *True Inheritance of the Atomic Bomb Experience*, which was distributed to all schools in Hiroshima to be used as material for peace education. Subsequently, activities, such as "Voice of A-bomb Survivors" and "Children Peace Summit", were launched creating spaces where students could gather to listen to A-bomb survivors' testimonies. Most recently, new programs like "Commitment to Peace" and "Peace Education Archives" have also been carried out. For high school students, the city offers more opportunities, such as dispatching students to NPT Review Conferences and its Preparatory Committees, to widen their knowledge on international peace affairs and develop their abilities in peace-building and peace-keeping.

Overall, throughout the development of peace education in Hiroshima and Japan, the focus had first been on anti-war and then shifted to anti-nuclear weapons. Specifically speaking, the mainstream of its peace education tends to emphasize the importance of negative peace, which means the absence of violence. Changes have been made due to the increasing globalization. Positive peace related content, such as multi-cultural communication, human rights education and environmental protection, is also included in the curriculum. However, as peace education in Japan is largely carried out in a knowledge-based manner, it is reported many students have the willingness to do something for peace but lack skills to put theories into practice.

Other Initiatives for Hiroshima Peace Education

In addition to the domestic popularization, efforts to promote Hiroshima peace education internationally are carried out too. In the 2001 Peace Declaration, the idea of establishing Hiroshima-Nagasaki Peace Study Courses in major universities around the world was put forward. The Cities of Hiroshima and Nagasaki, together with the Hiroshima Peace Culture Foundation, have long been working hard to encourage universities to launch the Hiroshima-Nagasaki Peace Study Courses. As of July 2022, the course has been established at 76 universities, including 52 in Japan and 24 overseas. Its aim is to educate the future generations about the inhumane and immoral nature of nuclear weapons through exploring the facts of the atomic bombings and sharing of the A-bomb experience from the survivors.

Apart from bringing Peace Study Courses into universities, the City of Hiroshima has held A-bomb exhibitions in and out of Japan since 1995, with its aim to raise a wider range of awareness of nuclear disarmament. Basically, the exhibitions comprise historical items, photo panels, and hibakusha testimonies. Sharing the same goal, the City of Hiroshima, collaborating with Hiroshima Peace Memorial Museum and Hiroshima National Peace Memorial Hall for the A-bomb Victims, also provides peace education for visitors through listening to A-bomb survivors' testimonies or watching A-bomb documentary films. Concerning the increasing number of tourists, the city integrates peace education into its tourism business and has created an online platform named "Hiroshima Peace Tourism" to help spread peace messages from Hiroshima across the world.

Another active actor that contributes to the promotion of nuclear disarmament centric peace education globally is civil society organizations. Take Peace Boat for example. It is a Japan-based international NGO, who offers a unique program of activities centered on experiential learning and intercultural communication through a passenger ship that travels around the world [Fig.5-2]. Serving as one of the 11 organizations from the International Steering Group of ICAN, it has for many years advocated and campaigned for a nuclear-free world, as well as offered support for all survivors of the nuclear chain.

Since 2008, Peace Boat has invited A-bomb survivors of Hiroshima and Nagasaki to participate in the Peace Boat Hibakusha Project, sharing their testimonies of the anti-humanitarian impact of nuclear weapons with people around the world during global voyages. As of 2019, over 170 hibakusha have traveled around the world giving personal testimonies about the effects of the atomic bombing and calling for nuclear disarmament in around 100 cities of more than 60 countries. Due to the COVID-19 pandemic, the project was changed to online testimony sessions to continue its calling on the elimination of nuclear weapons.

Fig.5-2 Peace Boat

Hiroshima Peace Research in Higher Education

The expansion of peace education is inseparable from the development of peace research. Having been recognized as an interdisciplinary effort aiming at achieving peace by peaceful means, Peace Studies includes research activities, where researchers develop new knowledge to enrich the sources; pedagogical activities, where teachers transmit knowledge and skills to students; and practical activities, where peace practitioners go to the conflicting zones for conflict transformation. Johan Galtung, the well-known peace scholar, demonstrates that peace research, peace education and peace action are intimately connected, and all three actors integrate into a natural whole.

Around the 1950s and the 1960s, following the institutionalization of Peace Studies in Europe and America, many peace research centers were established, delivering peace related books and journals. Subsequently, departments of peace studies were set up and courses on peace studies began to be taught in universities. From the end of the 1960s to the middle of the 1970s, a similar trend developed in Japan. In 1966, the Japan Peace Research Group (Nihon Heiwa Kenkyu Koudankai) was founded to facilitate the institutionalization of Peace Studies, which led to the establishment of Peace Studies Association of Japan (PSAJ) in 1973. Since then, PSAJ has played a leading role in encouraging and developing peace research in Japan.

Following the trend, in July 1975, the first academic research body focusing on Peace Studies based on Hiroshima's atomic bomb experience was established. Initially it was named the Institute for Peace Science, Hiroshima University (IPSHU), as a facility of Hiroshima University for the collection of data and research on peace science. In April 2018, the institute was renamed The Center for Peace, Hiroshima University (CPHU), with the aim to strengthen its role to promote peace research and peace education [Fig.5-3].

Fig.5-3 The office of The Center for Peace, Hiroshima University

Concerning peace research, CPHU focuses on two main themes: "Hiroshima Peace Research" (research on negative peace) and "Global Peace Research" (research on positive peace). "Hiroshima Peace Research" includes themes like aftermath effects of the atomic bombing and abolition of nuclear weapons, while "Global Peace Research" lays more emphasis on peace-building, human rights issues, and structural and environmental violence, etc. To encourage exchanges among peace institutions and peace researchers domestically and internationally, CPHU holds and facilitates joint research projects, annual international symposium, and research seminars, etc. For instance, in 1980, the Center held two study meetings monthly or bimonthly with the United Nation University (UNU) on the theme of peace and development.

Findings and papers from symposiums and research seminars have been selectively published in their own publications, in the form of research reports or newsletters. The Center also established an annual journal called *Hiroshima Peace Science* (*Hiroshima Heiwa Kagaku*), which has articles in both Japanese and English. To collect and build a comprehensive database on both Peace Studies and nuclear disaster, CPHU created its own library, which houses 10,000 scholarly books and over 60 academic journals in the field of Peace Studies.

In April 1998, another peace research body called Hiroshima Peace Institute (HPI) was established by the City of Hiroshima, as a research unit of Hiroshima City University (HCU). Like CPHU, HPI also places its focus on the elimination of nuclear weapons and the realization of achieving sustainable global peace. Most of its research findings are not only disseminated through academic publications and conference newsletters (online or printed), but also used in both undergraduate and graduate courses to promote peace education.

Whereas a bit different from CPHU, HPI pays more effort on the development of local and regional communities. In terms of regional cooperation, since its establishment, the institute has been collaborating with research institutions in Northeast Asia as well as one in Portugal. The two institutions in China are the Institute of Japan Studies at Liaoning University and the Department of Asian and International Studies at City University of Hong Kong.

As for its contribution to the local communities, every year in fall, HPI holds a lecture-based workshop series for citizens, introducing a wide range of social and international issues related to peace and conflict. Additionally, every winter there are public lecture series organized by international researchers to share their latest academic results with the residents. Both programs are held in the city on weekday evenings, which makes it easier for the public to attend. In 2015, HPI started a new program called the Hiroshima Peace Seminar. Basically, it is a summer intensive course for graduate students, researchers, civil servants, and media workers.

In April 2019, the Hiroshima City University launched its Graduate School of Peace Studies (Master's Degree Program), being the very first national university in Japan to establish a peace studies program. With its aim to serve as a global base for education and academic research for peace-building and peace-keeping, the two-year master program comprises some 30 subjects, largely related to the field of nuclear disarmament and international relations. In April 2021, a three-year doctoral program was also opened, comprising more advanced seminars on peace studies and international relations.

All in all, peace education and peace research in and from Hiroshima help to develop young generations' interest in broader peace issues and to spread peace messages of no more nuclear weapons widely. Nonetheless, both focuses are largely arising from Hiroshima's own atomic victimhood, which somewhat creates space for controversy like its mainstream peace movement does.

"Pacifism" without Peace

It is notable that Hiroshima city, together with many civil society organizations, has long paid their leading efforts across borders and generations to accomplish a world without nuclear weapons through peace movement and peace education. The achievements also help beautify Japan's image in the international community, primarily as a cultured and peace-loving nation. However, regarding the Hiroshima peace narrative, there are three major problems that deserve more attention. First, Japan seeks security under the U.S. nuclear umbrella and rejects to sign on TPNW despite its people's, mostly from Hiroshima and Nagasaki, tireless work in advocating nuclear disarmament as their moral responsibilities. Second, Hiroshima, the international city of peace, still holds its potential as a military city, being surrounded by both U.S. and Japanese military bases. Third, since the 1954 Lucky Dragon Incident, the Hiroshima-oriented peace activities have laid the focus on anti-nuclear weapons issues and kept avoiding touching upon Japan's war responsibility of its past aggression, which somehow narrows the possibilities of pursuing reconciliation with its neighboring nations in Asia.

Japan and Its Nuclear Dilemma

Because of the atomic bombings of Hiroshima and Nagasaki, there was always an anti-nuclear sentiment in Japan. But it did not reach its climax until the 1954 Lucky Dragon Incident, which paved its path to be a non-nuclear weapon country. Passed in 1955, the Atomic Energy Basic Law limits nuclear activity to peaceful purposes and constrains the weapon option. On 11 December 1967, Japan adopted the Three Non-Nuclear Principles of not possessing, not producing, and not permitting the introduction of nuclear weapons, in line with its post-war Peace Constitution. In 1970, Japan signed the NPT and ratified it in 1976. Japan has also played a leading role to promote nuclear disarmament in the international community, such as co-sponsoring the annual United Nations General Assembly resolution calling for the total elimination of nuclear weapons over the past 27 years.

However, during the Cold War, Japan came under the U.S. nuclear umbrella on the condition that it will not produce nuclear weapons. Though the primary object of the U.S. nuclear umbrella is to protect the U.S. itself, its allies can also benefit from the American nuclear capabilities. It is true that under this umbrella Japan cannot produce nuclear weapons, but the U.S. can, because the Anpo Treaty has ensured the U.S. almost free hands on the deployment of military forces in Japan. According to the historical findings provided by Nautilus Institute's East Asia Nuclear Policy Project, the U.S. routinely brought nuclear weapons into Japan during the Cold War despite Japan's non-nuclear policy and its public anti-nuclear sentiment.

Forced to choose between ignoring its own nuclear ban and confronting its most important ally, for several decades the Japanese Government has sacrificed its own non-nuclear policy to become involved in the U.S. nuclear weapons practices. Japan's official and firm rejection of signing the TPNW in 2017 was one of its commitments to this power-imbalanced relationship. With this treaty, signatories accept a prohibition from developing, testing, producing, stockpiling, transferring, and using or threatening to use nuclear weapons, as well as assisting other countries to engage in prohibited activities or seeking assistance from anyone engaged in actions that violate the treaty. In other words, signing onto this treaty means Japan would have to change its position toward the U.S nuclear umbrella, which is a bridge too far despite its own domestic principles.

On the other hand, Japan can construct its own nuclear weapons at will, withholding proper nuclear energy infrastructure and stockpiles. Japan's plutonium stockpile, according to the data released by the Japan Atomic Energy Commission, is about 47.3 tons of plutonium (as of the end of 2017), of which 36.7 tons is overseas (21.2 tons in the U.K. and 15.5 tons in France) and 10.5 tons in Japan. The only 10.5 tons of plutonium stockpiled in Japan is enough to make some 2,000 bombs. Although the demilitarization and the protection of the U.S. nuclear umbrella have led to a strong policy of non-weaponization of nuclear technology in Japan, in the face of the shifting strategic paradigm in Northeast Asia and the repeated demanding from the U.S. to pay more for the U.S. military operations (including maintaining its nuclear umbrella), many of Japan's conservative politicians and former military officials are now calling for a reversal of the policy.

As a matter of fact, 1954 was also the year when the Japanese Government began funding a nuclear research program. To smoothly carry out the program, it was urgent to suppress the fierce anti-nuclear sentiment among the public. In shifting the public opinion on nuclear energy, the idea of "Atoms for Peace" played a huge role. On 8 December 1953, to mask its nuclear weapons buildup, President Eisenhower delivered his "Atoms for Peace" speech at the United Nations, pledging to spread the benefits of peaceful atomic power at home and abroad. It was considered that Hiroshima could not be a more appropriate venue to advocate this "peaceful" idea. In January 1954, Bern Porter, an American scientist who had been involved in the Manhattan Project, spent three weeks in Hiroshima investigating the devastation and proposed the idea of "Atoms for Peace" to Mayor Hamai. U.S. Atomic Energy Commission Commissioner Thomas Murray also agreed, proclaiming, "it would be a dramatic and Christian gesture to construct a nuclear power plant in Japan, which could lift all of us far above the memory of the Hiroshima and Nagasaki atomic bombings".

As a result, Hiroshima was suggested to be the ideal city to locate the first electricity-producing nuclear power plant. In early 1955, the legislation to build a 60,000-kilowatt generating plant there was introduced, aiming to beautify the image of the atom as an instrument for electrical power rather than a killing weapon. In June, the U.S. and Japan signed an agreement to work together on research and development of atomic energy. In December, Japan passed the Atomic Energy Basic Law and established the Japan Atomic Energy Commission.

Since the strong anti-nuclear sentiment arose from the Lucky Dragon Incident, it was not easy to sell the "peaceful" idea to the Japanese people. When the Atoms for Peace Campaign was launched by the U.S. Embassy, U.S. Information Service (USIS), and Central Intelligence Agency (CIA), they turned to the *Yomiuri Shimbun Newspaper* and the Nippon Television Network for support. Eventually in November 1955, the Atoms for Peace Exhibit was successfully organized to welcome the atom back to Japan. After six weeks in Tokyo, the exhibit traveled to Hiroshima and six other cities. Together with relative films, lectures and articles, enormous success was achieved. It was reported that by the beginning of 1956, the peaceful use of atomic energy was gradually accepted by the Japanese populace.

The mainstream of Ban-the-Bomb Movement was no exception, so was the City of Hiroshima. The idea of "Atoms for Peace" was gradually approved by Mayor Hamai (with certain conditions), the *Chugoku Shimbun*, and the second Mayor Watanabe, etc. Around the middle of 1956, the Exhibit reached Hiroshima and was held in the Peace Memorial Park. Co-organized by Hiroshima city, Hiroshima prefecture, Hiroshima University, Hiroshima American Culture Center (ACC) and the *Chugoku Shimbun*, it lasted for about 3 weeks. In wanting the country to be a modern scientific-industrial power while lacking energy resources, the public allowed themselves to be convinced that nuclear power was safe and clean. Consequently, the Japanese nuclear power industry flourished in the 1960s and 1970s and continued to grow thereafter until the Fukushima nuclear disaster.

On 11 March 2011, a powerful tsunami was triggered by the Great East Japan Earthquake (Higashi Nihon Daishinsai), which caused severe damage to the Fukushima Daiichi Nuclear Power Plant in Okuma, Fukushima. It was considered the most destructive nuclear accident since the Chernobyl disaster in 1986. In the wake of the Fukushima disaster, public fears towards nuclear radiation exposure arose and objections against nuclear expansion grew rapidly. Japan, the nation that has experienced two atomic bombings and one nuclear disaster, must have known the danger of nuclear power better than many other nations. But due to its limited energy resources, Japan has heavily depended on this controversial energy and people have been benefiting from it for a long while. The nation is stuck in a nuclear dilemma, so do many other nations around the world. Until a more clean, safe, reliable, and affordable energy is invented, the dilemma will probably remain.

Hiroshima and Its Potential as a Military City

Speaking of military operations, if you look a bit further from the peace city, you will surprisingly find that Hiroshima is surrounded by two major military bases, Iwakuni Base and Kure Base. Iwakuni Base (or Marine Corps Air Station Iwakuni/MCAS Iwakuni) is some 34 kilometers away from Hiroshima and claimed to be one of the largest airbases in East Asia [Fig.5-4]. It is a Japan-U.S. joint military base, serving not only as the JMSDF base but also the United States Marine Corps (USMC) air station. Being a mission-ready air station, it can provide continuous base-operating support for tenant organizations and follow-on U.S. and Allied Forces during training, combat, or contingency operations throughout the Indo-Asia Pacific region.

Fig.5-4 An aerial view of Iwakuni Base, 28 April 2010

Fig.5-5 United States Army Kure Pier 6, November 2020

As for Kure Base, it is located some 20 kilometers away from Hiroshima [Fig.5-5]. In 2019, Kure Base officially became home port of the helicopter carrier JS Kaga—the biggest warship that Japan's navy has built since the end of World War II. Together with its sister ship the Izumo, Js Kaga was modified by Abe's Government to carry the U.S.-made F-35B stealth fighter jets [Fig.5-6]. When Abe was in office, he had been working for many years to strengthen Japan's military and expand its ability to use force, including pushing to amend the Peace Constitution to formally recognize the Japanese Self-Defense Forces. JS Kaga was indeed a good example in its effort on military buildup. In 2019, Prime Minister Abe invited President Trump to visit the warship during Trump's stay in Japan and announced the purchase of 105 U.S.-made F-35 fighters as Trump repeatedly criticized U.S. allies for not spending enough on their military buildup.

Fig.5-6 USMC F-35B Lightning II training flights at MCAS Iwakuni

Apart from the two major bases, there are several other military facilities encircling Hiroshima city, such as the Japan Ground Self-Defense Force Haramura Training Ground, Ground Self-Defense Force Kaita Base, U.S. Army Kawakami Ammunition Depot, U.S. Army Akizuki Ammunition Depot, and U.S. Army Hiro Ammunition Depot. It is undeniable that military bases and facilities have profound impacts on local economic growth, but in doing so it displays that Hiroshima city—the notable international city of peace—seems to remain as a military city as it was during the wartime period. All these military bases and facilities, together with several others stationed in Yokosuka, Nagasaki, and Okinawa, form a massive war preparation zone.

No More Hiroshima and No More...?

In the case of Japan, one of its central contested issues is to take responsibility for waging aggressive wars against its Asian neighbors in the past. However, throughout the Hiroshima-centric peace movement, reconciliation, the long-term process that needs careful examination of the past, has rarely been touched upon. Instead, the focus has long been on anti-nuclear weapons issues since the Hiroshima and Nagasaki atomic bombings had ever been recognized as Japan's national victimization. This way of considering the whole nation as a victim of war ultimately led to the popular idea that the victims were not responsible for the atrocities committed by the Imperial Japanese military forces against vast numbers of people in the Asia Pacific. To quote from Yuki Tanaka, a historian and political critic, "the collective sense of victimization led to a collective sense of irresponsibility".

In addition, the initial and official Hiroshima peace narrative also had a great impact on the formation of its peace movement. Peace scholars and researchers have addressed that peace has to do with the past, the present and the future. However, the Hiroshima peace narrative was mainly invented for the future. As it was discussed earlier, it was then approved by both the U.S. occupation forces and the Japanese Government, of whom the former wanted to dissociate Hiroshima's massive destruction from its dropping of the atomic bomb, and the latter sought to deny any causal relationship between the atomic bombing and Japan's aggression in Asia. In other words, this future-oriented peace narrative has trapped Japan in an unhealthy stance, where it has no choice but to depict itself as an innocent wartime victimized nation.

Consequently, Japan must forget certain years, such as the years of 1931 and 1941, but only remember the year of 1945 as its beginning of wartime history. Gradually, as Makoto Oda recalled in his writing: "In my case, for example, the Sino-Japanese War and the invasion of China are hardly included in the intellectual experiences of my childhood. When I think about World War II, I am at first conscious of the Pacific War. The same is true of the Japanese people. The Japanese people don't have much consciousness of having invaded China and tend to emphasize only the suffering they bore in the Pacific War. The invasion of China isn't part of it."

To avoid the mention of Japan's wartime aggression, especially the surprise attack on Pearl Harbor, the atomic bombing of Hiroshima was interpreted as a natural disaster that accidentally attacked Hiroshima. Under this setting, it is unquestionable that Japan cannot seek reconciliation with the U.S on the atomic bombings. Because when it did ask for compensation, the 1941 Pearl Harbor Attack would be brought up straightaway. This would not only justify the dropping of the atomic bombs, but also destroy Japan's long-standing image of being a peace-loving nation. In this regard, the Hiroshima authorities also made a lot of efforts. For example, the fact that it was the U.S. who dropped the atomic bomb on Hiroshima has never been clearly pointed out in every year's Peace Declaration since it was initiated in 1947.

Nevertheless, some argue that Obama—the first sitting U.S. president's visit to the once-destroyed city on 27 May 2016 could be interpreted as a significant sign of U.S.-Japan reconciliation. Ranked as the top news of that year in Japan, it was said that President Obama, together with Prime Minister Abe, toured the Peace Memorial Museum and laid a wreath at the A-bomb Cenotaph. The 17-minute speech advocating the elimination of nuclear weapons delivered by Obama was also claimed to be noteworthy and powerful, even though he was holding a nuclear button while speaking.

In the remarks, Obama depicted the atomic bombing as a natural disaster and expressed no words of apology, yet his presence was reported to be highly welcomed by most Japanese people, including a small group of A-bomb survivors who were carefully selected by the Japanese Government to attend the ceremony.

In fact, the stay of President Obama and Prime Minister Abe in the peace museum was less than 10 minutes and in Hiroshima city was less than one hour and a half. Instead, they spent more hours in Iwakuni, inspecting the MCAS Iwakuni. Additionally, one month before Obama's visit, another Okinawa rape incident occurred, where a 20-year-old Okinawan woman was raped and murdered by a U.S. military sailor. A strong anti-U.S. sentiment once again arose from Okinawa, which eventually led to a small-scale demonstration against President Obama's visit in the peace park on the day when Obama was there.

President Obama's visit to Hiroshima also sparked a controversy in the United States. In general, those who supported his visit believed that it was a significant gesture to reaffirm U.S.'s commitment to world peace. On the other hand, opponents of the visit argued that it was unnecessary and wrong for Obama to visit Hiroshima, either intentionally or unintentionally, to express regret over the dropping of the atomic bombs, because it was Japan who first launched the war of aggression and the attack on Pearl Harbor. Thus, it was necessary and correct to use the atomic bombs to end the war as soon as possible.

Officially, the White House also clarified that Obama's historic visit should not be interpreted as an apology, but a forward-looking signal for his ambition of realizing the goal of a planet with no nuclear weapons. Strictly speaking, Obama's dropping in on Hiroshima may only be seen as the countries' mutual commitment to reducing nuclear weapons, rather than a gesture of apology on the use of the atomic bombs. Ironically, in October of the same year, Japan and the United State both opposed the resolution adopted by the First Committee of the UN General Assembly to start negotiations of establishing a "nuclear ban treaty".

In response to Obama's visit to Hiroshima, in December of the same year, Prime Minister Abe visited Pearl Harbor and offered his condolences to the victims of Japan's attack on the base. This time it was praised by President Obama, who called Prime Minister Abe's presence a "historic gesture" that showed the power of reconciliation. As a matter of fact, Abe did not apologize for the attack but said: "We must never repeat the horrors of war again... it was important to show respect even to a former enemy." Even if it was a "historic gesture of reconciliation" as President Obama interpreted, it can merely be captured as Japan-U.S. reconciliation over Pearl Harbor Attack, but certainly not over the U.S.'s dropping the atomic bombs on Hiroshima and Nagasaki.

However, there is no doubt that President Obama's visit to Hiroshima and Prime Minister Abe's trip to Pearl Harbor further consolidated the Japan-U.S. relationship and pleased many Japanese and Americans. But how about the people in Asia?

> President Obama's visit to Hiroshima was welcomed by the Japanese, but what would the responses from the victimized Asian countries be? For most of the Japanese, they take it for granted that "No More Hiroshima" and "No More Nagasaki" is the start of the peace movement. However, chasing back to the history of Japan being a perpetrator to Asian countries, especially China and Korea, voices like "No More Nanjing" are nowhere to be heard.
>
> —A Japanese journalist (May 2016)

Accordingly, voices calling for Japan's Prime Minister to visit Nanjing also appeared. Like the Hiroshima visit and the Pearl Harbor trip, even though there were no words directly offering an apology, the presence of the leaders itself would have some symbolic meaning for reconciliation over the painful wartime history in between.

Unfortunately, the notorious textbook issue, Japanese leaders' continuous visits to Yasukuni Shrine and the frequent denials of the Nanjing Massacre and the "Comfort Women" issue keep poisoning the regional relations from time to time. Looking back at the development of the Hiroshima originated peace movement, reconciliation between Japan and its neighboring countries has rarely been part of it. It is understandable that Hiroshima lays its emphasis on anti-nuclear weapons issues considering its special status quo as a once devastated city by the atomic bombing. But before the day of the atomic bombing, the city had been a major military capital and played an active role in Imperial Japan's aggressive wars and colonization of other Asian nations and regions. The conventional aerial bombings of other cities across the nation, as well as the atomic bombings of Hiroshima and Nagasaki arrived in the next stage of Japan's imperialism.

To conceal its past aggression and colonization, Japan also granted itself "the only A-bombed nation" while recognizing the Hiroshima and Nagasaki atomic bombings as its national victimization. Seiji Imahori, a Japanese scholar in Chinese history and an anti-nuclear activist, once criticized:

> *In Japan, everyone from successive prime ministers to the Communist Party has repeatedly declared us "the only nation ever to have been atom-bombed" (yuiitsu no hibakukoku). Putting aside for the moment the fact that they were forgetting the American soldiers who were exposed in the Nevada tests and the Pacific aboriginals of Bikini and Eniwetok, I feel that this declaration is replete with the single-minded assertion that Japanese were the victims of the atomic bomb. Why did the citizens of Hiroshima and Nagasaki become victims? Do the Japanese hold no responsibility whatsoever? Can you state simply that the citizens of Hiroshima were injured as if they one day suddenly met with some natural disaster?*

Since the 1980s, "the only A-bombed nation" has frequently been used in the Peace Declarations annually delivered by Mayors of Hiroshima and widely appeared in the media and other occasions, both official and unofficial. Outwardly, this title consolidates Japan's responsibility to call for nuclear disarmament, but in the meantime, it masks the responsibilities of both Hiroshima and Japan as an aggressor during the wartime as the above quotation from Seiji Imahori reads. In addition, it invisiblizes the existence of many non-Japanese A-bomb victims, among whom many were forced laborers from the Korean Peninsula while some were from China and several other nations.

Overall, for the Japanese public, the perception of being "the only A-bombed nation" has formed an important part of their collective memory of the war. As a result, anti-nuclear weapons became the mainstream of the postwar peace movements in Japan. From a humanitarian perspective, the logic seems not controversial. However, "the only A-bombed nation" victim identity solidifies the public opinions that "the war was imposed from the outside and that the Japanese people were only victims themselves". Taking the stance of being victims only prevents Japan and its people from seeing and acknowledging the sufferings they brought to the other nations, which in turn makes the process of reconciliation difficult to carry out.

From Negative Peace to Positive Peace

The dual concepts of negative peace and positive peace have been touched upon several times in the previous sessions, and here they will be used to examine the peace narrative of Hiroshima. Theoretically, negative peace is the absence of violence and war, or a state that can be achieved by violent means and still has unrest. In contrast, positive peace is the absence (or reduction) of violence and war and the presence of "positive components" that enable and sustain peaceful growth and peaceful change. As for "positive components", Galtung explains them as the presence of equity and harmony, including the presence of restorative relationships, social systems that serve the needs of society, and the elimination of structural violence. In other words, positive peace is peace achieved by peaceful means. In Peace Studies, the dual concepts are helpful to facilitate the understanding of peace as a dynamic process where actions are taken to de-escalate and transform conflicts.

Looking back on the status quo of Hiroshima, being surrounded by military bases with its main-stream peace movement largely focusing on the nuclear disarmament (peace as the absence of violence) and almost silent about the existence of military bases (peace that can be achieved by violent means), it is fair to interpret the peace narrative of Hiroshima as negative peace. If we kept entrapped in the duality of self and the other, constantly seeing the other as a threat to the existence of us, the notion of strengthening one's military force to secure its territory would continue functioning.

However, for today's globalized world, we shall try to look beyond Darwin's "survival of the fittest" theory and search for creative and revolutionary ideas, such as "survival of the most cooperative", which might have great potential to make our planet a better and healthier space to coexist. For example, regarding conflicting issues between or among nations, a more peaceful way of having constructive dialogue rather than the utilization of military power, should be encouraged to kill the possibility of waging war against our human nature and mother nature. This is what has been defined as positive peace and is what Hiroshima needs to pay more attention to. Although knowledge on positive peace has been integrated into the peace education curriculum, since it is conducted in a knowledge-based way of teaching, many of the theories have not yet been well practiced.

One of the "positive components" contributing to the building up of positive peace, as it was mentioned previously, is to restore relationships. While concerning the reconciliation process, as many scholars of peace and reconciliation have emphasized, it is an overly complex process that needs truth, justice, peace, and mercy. It would not be possible until we were awakened and liberated to see all human beings as one tribe, regardless of race, religion, nationality, and social status. That is, to restore our broken relationships, all involved parties, regardless of being the former perpetrator or victim, need to make efforts and changes.

Fig.5-7 From left to right, Dr. Yasunori Takazane, director of the museum, Akira Kawasaki, a representative of Peace Boat and Oliver Stone, an American film director, were looking at the exhibition on non-Japanese A-bomb survivors (mainly Korean and Chinese) in the Oka Masaharu Memorial Nagasaki Peace Museum, 10 August 2013

In the context of Hiroshima, before being victimized its responsibility of being a perpetrator should also be taken into consideration, not only in its peace movement but also peace education. In this regard, Nagasaki, the city that also experienced the atomic bombing like Hiroshima, seems to take the lead. For instance, Oka Masaharu Memorial Nagasaki Peace Museum (Oka Masaharu Kinen Nagasaki Heiwa Shiryoukan) [Fig.5-7] has long been an educational base for passing on Japan's wartime history as an aggressor, including its colonization of Korean Peninsula, invasion of China (Nanjing Massacre and Unit 731) and the rest of Asia, as well as condemnation of the emperor-system fascism, etc. (Sharing a similar spirit, Kyoto Museum for World Peace, Ritsumeikan University also lays its focus on

Japan's aggressive past.) The museum was built by civilian volunteers, in memory of Masaharu Oka (1918-1994), who initiated peace movements calling Japan to take its full responsibility of being a wartime aggressor from a very early stage. In 2000, the museum established a friendship with the Memorial Hall of the Victims in Nanjing Massacre by Japanese Invaders in Nanjing, China. Through the images and material provided by the Memorial Hall, the museum presents a vivid depiction of the Nanjing Massacre. In 2002, the museum also initiated a program called "China-Japan Friendship—Wings of Hope" (Niichu Yukou Kibou no Tsubasa), encouraging Japanese students to visit China and learn history through local field trips.

Very recently, a similar effort was also made from Hiroshima to restore grassroots relationships between China and Japan. In 2015, organized jointly by Asia and Pacific Alliance of YMCAs (APAY) and YMCAs respectively of Hiroshima, Nanjing and Daegu, the 6th YMCA Peace Forum was held in Nanjing. YMCA staff, volunteers, and the youth from the three countries explored the possibilities of building trusting relationships through learning and experiencing both positive and negative histories that are shared among them. Northeast Asia Regional Peacebuilding Institute (NARPI), a Korea-based institute aiming to promote peace in the region, is also offering similar programs yearly in different places, such as Hiroshima and Nanjing. Other civilian initiatives from Hiroshima have also been put forward. For instance, a small bunch of teachers are trying to create their own peace education curriculum, integrating Japan's aggressive past into the atomic bombing centric teachings.

"Small is beautiful," says Gandhi. If Hiroshima could be more as proactive as its role played in leading the abolishment of nuclear weapons to deeply reflect upon its past and take the lead to initiate dialogic trust-building and reconciliation processes with its Asian neighbors, such as with China, it would not only benefit the countries involved but also the whole region in many ways. Specifically, Hiroshima could start bridging Nanjing to create a trusting relationship in between through sharing and healing the historical wounds that we human beings have experienced and never want to experience anymore. Mercifully, a friendly connection between the two cities has already been built thanks to Prof. Liu Cheng, Chairholder of UNESCO Chair on Peace Studies, Nanjing University and Prof. Noriyuki Kawao, Director of The Center for Peace, Hiroshima University.

In addition, similar initiatives seeking to promote China-Japan relationships at the grassroots level have been carried out in the academic field. Take the China-Japan Dialogue on Peace Studies for example. The proposal was first brought forward by Prof. Akihiko Kimijima, then Chairperson of the Program Committee of PSAJ to Prof. Liu Cheng of Nanjing University early in 2015. With support from the Charhar Institute, Prof. Liu met and discussed with Prof. Kimijima and several other PSAJ members in May during his stay in Tokyo for a conference where he was invited to deliver a speech. Both sides expressed their sincere wishes to build relationships with scholars who share the same spirit. Thus, mutual consent was quickly reached, and the first dialogue was held in October of the same year in Beijing. Jointly organized by Charhar Institute and PSAJ, the first dialogue focused on the past, the present and the future of China-Japan relations, through which a friendship based on mutual respect and trust was established between Chinese and Japanese scholars.

To deepen and enrich the friendship in between, the second dialogue took place in Nanjing in 2017, with support not only from the Charhar Institute and PSAJ, but also the Institute of Nanjing Massacre History and International Peace and the Institute for Peace of Nanjing University. Scholars from China and Japan, together with Norwegian scholar Galtung, discussed cooperation between China and Japan on the development of Peace Studies. Following the same spirit, the third dialogue was held in Ritsumeikan University Osaka Ibaraki Campus in 2019. The focus continued to be exploring the possibility of China-Japan cooperation on Peace Studies, but at the same time, regional issues related to peace and conflict were also discussed.

Due to the COVID-19 pandemic, the very recent two dialogues of 2020 and 2021 were held online by the International Relations Committee of PSAJ and UNESCO Chair on Peace Studies, Nanjing University. Different from the previous ones, these two dialogues offered more space to welcome university students from both countries to exchange ideas on peace and conflict related issues that are still destabilizing the relationship between China and Japan. To have youth lead and participate in the dialogue brings hope for the future.

Even though the pandemic has changed the world dramatically, peace cannot wait. To continue the dialogue is of great importance to facilitate mutual understanding especially during this turbulent time. It is true that effort from the ground is small, but "a single spark can start a prairie fire". Hopefully, the ongoing journey to reconciliation and peace from the grassroots will go on smoothly, liberating us all from deeply rooted enmity and division.

Conclusion

While walking through the long history of Hiroshima's ups and downs, there arose multiple sentiments. There was peacefulness and tranquility when Hiroshima was simply a City of Water, where residents enjoyed a harmonious life with the other human fellows and with mother nature. Following the urbanization of the city and the development of its industrial business, excitement and anticipation arrived. However, during the Meiji Period, the idea of "Leave Asia, Enter Europe" was invented, which strengthened Imperial Japan's intention of expansionism overseas, especially in Asia.

Consequently, at the dawn of the Meiji Period, Hiroshima city took on national importance, functioning as one of the few essential military cities of Imperial Japan where military installations were built one after another, and military troops were sent off one after another. As Japan's aggressive war progressed, military supplies became the initial priority of the city and civilians had to make daily sacrifices of whatever it took in support of the war effort during the war. On 6 August 1945, war brought further destruction. An atomic bomb was dropped on the city by the U.S., which made it a land of victimhood in a flash. Fear and rage mounted in every corner of the city.

Mercifully, trees and flowers began to sprout soon after the atomic bombing, which brought great vitality and hope to the people and the city. Through the efforts generally from the grassroots citizen groups all round the world, the city was able not only to rebuild the damaged areas but also to reinvent itself as a city of peace. Strategically using its unique A-bomb victimization, Hiroshima's calling for the elimination of nuclear weapons has gained wide recognition and resonation. However, the narrative of Hiroshima peace tends to be a future-oriented term that supports the ideology of "starting over" based on a deliberate amnesia about the wartime experience of Japan being a victimizer. As a result, reconciliation with its former Asian neighbors has rarely been addressed along the way.

"Reconciliation is a process that never ends. Reconciliation is not the process of forgetting, but an attitude to the other man", is the essence that Hiroshima, and many other war-torn cities can learn from the model of German-Polish reconciliation. To reconcile is to heal. It has been longed for by many human societies, including Hiroshima. As I walked around the modern-day Hiroshima, it is a prosperous and lively city seemingly no different from any other Japanese cities. There are featureless offices and apartment blocks, ubiquitous convenience stores and chain coffee shops. Even the Peace Memorial Park that is elegant and solemn in the day, is surrounded by flashing neon lights in the evening where people are enjoying their nightlife. After all, life must go on. It is true that the gloom of the past seems to be far away, but hidden conflicts generated by past wounds remain unreconciled and are doubtlessly going to impact the future. Only when the past is integrated into the present, will we be more capable of heading towards a harmonious future.

Main Bibliography

1. Alperovitz, G., The Decision to Use the Atomic Bomb, Vintage Books, 1996.

2. Buruma, I., Wages of Guilt: Memories of War in Germany and Japan, Farrar Straus & Giroux, 1994.

3. Cho, H., Hiroshima Peace Memorial Park and the Making of Japanese Postwar Architecture, Journal of Architectural Education, 66(1), 2012, pp.72-83.

4. Cook, H. T. & T. F. Cook, Japan at War: An Oral History, The New Press, 1992.

5. Dower, J. W., Embracing Defeat: Japan in the Aftermath of World War II, Penguin Group (CA), 2000.

6. Galtung, J., Peace by Peaceful Means: Peace and Conflict, Development and Civilization, SAGE, 1996.

7. Hiroshima and Nagasaki: The Physical, Medical, and Social Effects of the Atomic Bombings, The Committee for the Compilation of Materials on Damage Caused by the Atomic Bombs in Hiroshima and Nagasaki, ed., Iwanami Shoten, 1981.

8. Hiroshima Reconstruction and Peacebuilding Research Project, Learning from Hiroshima's Reconstruction Experience: Reborn from the Ashes, Hiroshima Prefecture and the City of Hiroshima, 2014. https://hiroshimaforpeace.com/en/wp-content/uploads/sites/2/2019/09/189227.pdf

9. Kingston, J., Renewing and Reframing Hiroshima, The Aisa-Pacific Journal: Japan Focus, 17(15), 2019.

10. Kosakai, Y. & A. R. Ramseyer, Hiroshima Peace Reader (A. Tashiro, M. Tashiro & R. R. Ramseyer, Trans.), Hiroshima Peace Culture Foundation, 2017.

11. Orr, J. J., The Victim as Hero: Ideologies of Peace and National Identity in Postwar Japan, University of Hawaii Press, 2001.

12. Scott, B. & M. Kasai, Two Pilgrims Meet: In Search of Reconciliation between China and Japan, New Generation Publishing, 2016.

13. Tanaka, Y., Photographer Fukushima Kikujiro — Confronting Images of Atomic Bomb Survivors (写真家福島菊次郎——被曝者の映像に直面する), The Aisa-Pacific Journal: Japan Focus, 9(43), 2011.

14. The Spirit of Hiroshima: An Introduction to the Atomic Bomb Tragedy (ヒロシマ を世界に), Hiroshima Peace Memorial Museum, 2019.

15. Treat, J. W., Writing Ground Zero: Japanese Literature and the Atomic Bomb, University of Chicago Press, 1996.

16. Vogel, E. F., China and Japan: Facing history, Harvard University Press, 2019.

17. Webel, C. & J. Galtung, Handbook of Peace and Conflict Studies, Routledge, 2007.

18. Zwigenberg, R., Hiroshima: The Origins of Global Memory Culture, Cambridge University Press, 2014.

19. 福島菊次郎『写らなかった戦後 ヒロシマの嘘』、現代人文社、2003 年。

20. 広島原爆医療史編集委員会『広島原爆医療史』、広島原爆障害対策協議会、1961 年。

21. 広島市『広島新史：歴史編』、1984 年。

22. 広島市・長崎市原爆災害誌編委員会『広島・長崎の原爆災害』、岩波書店、1979 年。

23. 現代思想 8 月号『＜広島＞の思想——いくつもの戦後史』、青土社、2016 年。

24. 権赫泰『平和なき「平和主義」：戦後日本の思想と運動 (鄭栄桓訳)』、法政大学出版局、2016 年。

25. 中沢啓治『「ヒロシマ」の空白：中沢家始末記』、日本図書センター、1987 年。

26. 岡田黎子『絵で語る子どもたちの太平洋戦争——毒ガス島・ヒロシマ・少国民』、文芸社、2013年。

27. 相馬一成『置いてきた毒ガス「母と子でみる」』、草の根出版会、1997年。

28. 田中利幸・ピーターカズニック『原発とヒロシマ「原子力平和利用」の真相』、岩波書店、1997年。

29. 步平:《跨越战后:日本的战争责任认识》,北京:社会科学文献出版社,2011年。

30. 冯玮:《日本通史》,上海:上海社会科学院出版社,2008年。

31. 刘成:《和平学》,南京:南京出版社,2006年。

32. 刘成、[德]埃贡·施皮格尔:《全球化世界的和平建设:图解和平学》,北京:人民出版社,2015年。

33. [英]巴兹尔·斯考特、[日]葛西实:《探寻中日和解之旅》,李琳莉、刘双双译,南京:南京师范大学出版社,2018年。

34. [英]大卫·巴迪:《日本帝国的终结》,徐莉娜、岳玉庆、曲芳丽译,青岛:青岛出版社,2013年。

Afterword

It was a summer night in 2019 that my interest in Hiroshima was ignited. It may sound inconceivable, but it was Nanjing that drove me to learn about Hiroshima. On the day, my friend from Nepal and I paid a visit to the Memorial Hall of the Victims in Nanjing Massacre by Japanese Invaders and Nanjing Museum of the Site of Lijixiang Comfort Stations. Both weighed heavily on our hearts and bodies. Back to the hotel, being physically and mentally exhausted, we both collapsed on our beds. After a moment of silence, she said, "I've never heard of the Nanjing Massacre, and it didn't appear in our history textbooks. But we had plenty of learning on the Hiroshima and Nagasaki atomic bombings!"

Traumatic memories of massive suffering happening anywhere are worth remembering by everywhere. When a wounded city's memory is integrated into the shared human memory, our understanding of one specific human suffering is more likely to go beyond certain politically and culturally framed norms. Nanjing was once a devastated city, just as Hiroshima was after the atomic bombing. But "how can Hiroshima city so successfully restore and reconstruct itself from ashes and transform into a notable city of peace?" It was the question that came to my mind at that moment and is also the question at the heart of this book. Bearing the wonder in mind, I joined the writing team for the Hiroshima volume in September and thereafter started my journey exploring Hiroshima. Through both experiential and non-experiential learning about Hiroshima, I was able to accomplish this volume. The entire process, to me, was a transformative and liberating experience, where I became increasingly aware of the fact that human-caused war has long been one of the major factors that continue ruining our relationships with our brothers and sisters and with our mother nature.

Today, in Northeast Asia most of us enjoy a comparatively peaceful living space where there is no direct war. However, our relationships that were broken by the dark past remain unrestored, and it continues to generate conflicts that destabilize the region. To make heart-to-heart relationship restoration happen, a mutual acknowledgement of the historical trauma shared by us human beings is very essential. In the case of China-Japan relations, bridging Nanjing and Hiroshima may be a challenging but creative start for both to cultivate mutual understanding and mutual trust in between.

As a matter of fact, both trauma healing and relationship restoration are long-term and never-ending processes, but only when the wounds are healed and the relationships are restored, can we break the cycle of violence and coexist in harmony. In the meantime, we shall also remember that we share many positive histories, which have long been deeply rooted in our way of living, thinking, and flourishing. They are the rich sources that unite us all as brothers and sisters in one human family.

All in all, it is impossible for me to thank all the many people who have made this book possible. But I cannot fail to mention some who have played a major part in bringing this volume to life. Particularly, I would like to express my gratitude to Prof. Liu Cheng, for his main guidance and kind invitation to have me write the volume. My special appreciation also goes to Dr. Kazuyo Yamane, who was the first to read the entire manuscript carefully and patiently and offer constructive comments that improved the quality of the volume; and to Prof. Kyoko Okumoto, my mentor, for her love and patience, understanding and support along the way.

Grateful thanks also go to Wang Xiaoyang, who contributed greatly at the earlier stages in making the publication possible and made the Chinese version available based on this English edition and its material; and to the main editors Wang Yaqiong, Xiang Lei, Zheng Haiyan, for their careful review and proofreading in making the volume well-organized and easily comprehensible for readers to enjoy.

Last but certainly not the least, my deepest and heartfelt gratitude goes to my beloved family, especially to my parents and elder sister, for their unconditional love and all the sacrifice they have made on my behalf; and to my dearest friends, Susmita Bastola, Cristina Cabrejas Artola, Nikolas Michael Krause, Suyeon Kang, Satoko Oka Norimatsu, Junko Hattori, Marcin Damek, Aya Kasai, Masae Yuasa, Egon Spiegel, Huang Muyu, Zhou Yunao and many more, for their agape and company.

Due to various limitations, this slender volume could not cover more detailed information about Hiroshima and its peace initiatives, but I hope that readers would find something meaningful from it.

May the world be a BELOVED FAMILY!

For Photo Credits Please Refer to